Gypsy

Gypsy

THE ART OF THE TEASE

LIBRARY
FRANKLIN PIERCE UNIVERSITY
RINDGE, NH 03461

Rachel Shteir

YALE UNIVERSITY PRESS   NEW HAVEN & LONDON

Copyright © 2009 by Rachel Shteir.

All rights reserved.

This book may not be reproduced, in whole or in part, including illustrations,
in any form (beyond that copying permitted by Sections 107 and 108 of the
U.S. Copyright Law and except by reviewers for the public press),
without written permission from the publishers.

Set in Janson type by Integrated Publishing Solutions.
Printed in the United States of America.

Library of Congress Cataloging-in-Publication Data
Shteir, Rachel, 1964–
Gypsy : the art of the tease / Rachel Shteir.
p.   cm.—(Icons of America)
Includes bibliographical references and index.
ISBN 978-0-300-12040-0 (hardcover : alk. paper)
1. Lee, Gypsy Rose, 1914–1970.   2. Stripteasers—United States—Biography.
I. Title.
PN2287.L29S58 2009
792.702′8092—dc22
[B]
2008040303

6-H-5/11

A catalogue record for this book is available from the British Library.

This paper meets the requirements of ANSI/NISO Z39.48-1992
(Permanence of Paper).
It contains 30 percent postconsumer waste (PCW) and is certified
by the Forest Stewardship Council (FSC).

10 9 8 7 6 5 4 3 2 1

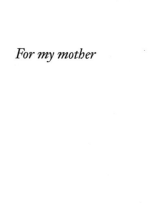

For my mother

I wanted to do business faster than the ordinary
mercantile transactions would admit.
—P. T. Barnum

Contents

Contents

Gypsy

"Particles, Legends, Romance"

Before the woman who became known as Gypsy Rose Lee arrived in New York in 1930, striptease took place more frequently on tables in saloon backrooms or in whorehouses than on Broadway or in Hollywood. The police raided the burlesque theaters where strippers performed and arrested them for indecent exposure. Judges determined whether their dances violated obscenity laws and sentenced them to jail time. No one wrote about striptease in chic and serious literary magazines. Society matrons and debutantes never giggled at a striptease (nor tried to do one). Nor did Broadway lyricists, Russian choreographers, or Hollywood screenwriters satirize taking it off.

After Gypsy's triumph, striptease became more than a crime or a vice. It was now an ironic diversion for middle-class and wealthy women, a sly commentary on the rags-to-riches myth, the sort of hoax that the *New Yorker* could write about as a universal ideal. After Gypsy, choreographers and lyricists punctuated the ballets and musicals with stripteases. Novelists used the stripper's character as a metaphor for American life's small injustices and hypocrisies. Comedians impersonated strippers and told tales about their dubious pasts. Striptease became a representative American act. Getting naked revealed an American truth. Stars and Stripes and Striptease forever.

Perhaps it is too much to pin all of these accomplishments on one woman, or to make the claim that this woman's striptease (or any striptease) was iconic. But Gypsy was the only stripper of her era—of any era—to become a household name, to write detective novels and plays, or to inspire a musical and four memoirs (one her own), a portrait by Max Ernst, and a variety of roses. Moreover, she was the only stripper whom intellectuals, bankers, socialites, and ordinary Americans adored.

How did she do it? For one thing, she turned striptease into what the scholar Robert Snyder described as "respectable thrills," meaning vaudeville acts teetering between prurience and good behavior. That Gypsy could make the act of undressing into such a thrill makes her a girl P. T. Barnum would be proud of in the now-you-see-it-now-you-don't razzle-dazzle twentieth century American showbiz world.

Whereas men in this world used patriotic songs or feats of

daring to command attention and applause, and to reveal their identities, Gypsy used striptease. She transformed stripping into something more than the banal physical act of taking off her clothes by making it into a fable about her life.

Americans did not universally applaud Gypsy for her efforts. If one aspect of her status as an icon rests on admiration of her leap from rags to riches doing something as naughty as stripping, another depends on outrage at the same. During her lifetime, re-formers and politicians not only continued to advocate for outlaw-ing striptease, they blamed Gypsy for promoting it. It disgusted them.

But a puritanical attitude toward striptease is ultimately doomed. For one, the physical act of taking it off is associated, however loosely, with self-revelation—an American motif since our nation's founding. If Gypsy's rise struck reformers as im-moral, to many writers, artists, and ordinary Americans it proved that fun and liberation from Victorian ideas had won. Gypsy: Robber Baroness of Undressing; American Libertine; Glorious Fake. This was also the first era in which people were, to use Daniel Boorstin's conceit, known for being well known. That Gypsy started as a stripper and then became a joke, a millionaire, a writer, a legend, a brand, a mother, a saleswoman, and a recluse demonstrates her status as an icon, if taking off her clothes for the American elite while making fun of them fails to accomplish this.

I had been mulling over Gypsy's permutations and complications for ten years when, in 2004, I set off on a tour for my first book, *Striptease: The Untold History of the Girlie Show.* Gypsy had lurked at the heart of that book, although she ultimately played a relatively small role in it. What intrigued me was this: thirty-some years after Gypsy's death, despite women's liberation, the sexual revolution, and modern pornography's ubiquity, her striptease and personae still interest American women as a physical act, a metaphor for self-revelation, a popular art, and a way to immorality.

What was Gypsy revealing, really? She taunted her audiences and readers, implying that she was about to tell all and then changing her mind. She did this in part by casting doubt on her own story's credibility; for example, she admitted that she stripped for just fifty weeks altogether. And then she took it back. In her act she seemed to veer away from admitting she was a fraud. If what she said was untrue, she could modify it. She saw herself as a work in progress.

So Gypsy's striptease was no "ordinary" one by the standards of the day. It was less about sex than it was about class. Rather than reveal her flesh, Gypsy, chatting about high culture, disguised herself. She took off a few pieces of clothing with studied hauteur. She was not the Circe of undressing—she was, as I have written elsewhere, its Dorothy Parker.

Long after Gypsy stopped stripping, she continued to mime taking it off, promising to reveal long after she had nothing left to reveal, teasing the audience that somewhere in the folds of her gowns lurked a new place of discovery. But ultimately Gypsy was too savvy (or too stingy) to give away new secrets.

All of this inspired (and sometimes infuriated) writers. Among the most memorable of striptease's describers is Roland Barthes, who, in 1957, the same year that Gypsy's memoir was published in America, characterized it as "particles of eroticism" "transplant[ing] the body into legend and romance."

I don't know if Gypsy counted Barthes among her favorite authors, as she did Proust. But she would have agreed that taking off her clothes in public could be understood as both metaphor and social reality.

In our era, thanks to Gypsy, striptease has come to be discussed in two ways: it is either an empowering event or an anxiety-making one. It either liberates women or oppresses them. As in her era, striptease performers still argue about how much they should take off. (And how much they are taking off, which is not always the same question.) Also as in Gypsy's era, when ex-stripper Anna Nicole Smith's sudden (and allegedly mysterious) death in 2007 attracted more news coverage than that devoted to any other story except the Iraqi war, some commentators interpreted it as a sign of our culture's decadence.

A main difference between Gypsy's time and our own is supposed to be that women (by which is meant white, middle-class women) have other options. But when a woman who does not need to strip (for money) still strips, there is thought to be something distasteful about it, as when Diablo Cody, who began life as Brook Busey Hunt, wrote *Candy Girl: A Year in the Life of an Unlikely Stripper*, a memoir about stripping in Minneapolis. The following year she wrote the screenplay for *Juno* (and won an Academy Award for her effort), and critics applauded and attacked, which demonstrates the hold that striptease has on the American psyche. Today women continue to write about their experiences stripping. Some take cardio-striptease classes, where they gyrate, shimmy, and lose weight. A few brave souls install striptease poles in their bedrooms. I strip, therefore I am.

Strippers maintain their own listservs, blogs, unions, and Web sites, and they create and sell their own CDs, magazines, and t-shirts. The Burlesque Hall of Fame crowns "Miss Exotic World" at a yearly contest, held most recently at The Palms in Las Vegas.

The idea that striptease divided the sexes continues to haunt us as well. Back in Gypsy's era, some writers worried that taking off one's clothes in public for money would bring down Western civilization or at least marriage as we know it. In 1935 John Erskine, literary scholar, light novelist, colleague of Mark van Doren, composer, and Juilliard's first president, complained that at a striptease performance the guy never gets the girl.

A Marxist version of Erskine's sentiment appeared shortly after Gypsy retired. In his 1960 essay "The Socratic Strip," Umberto Eco reckoned that striptease was bad for the proletariat. "The striptease unconsciously teaches the spectator, who seeks and accepts frustration, that the means of production are not within his reach." In the twentieth century's last decade, some Third Wave Feminists seized upon striptease as an "empowering" act, arguing that women should toss bras offstage, not burn them. The most recent backlash against striptease charges that the eager young feminists who say they are expressing themselves while taking it off are girls in voyeurs' clothing. In *Female Chauvinist Pigs: Women and the Rise of Raunch Culture* Ariel Levy writes, "Some odd things were happening to people in my social life, too. People I knew (female people) liked going to strip clubs."

Gypsy, whose early admirers called her "The Queen of Striptease," the way Ella Fitzgerald's called her "The Queen of Jazz," launched Americans into this fascination the way JFK launched

Americans into space. The pioneer of undressing sheds light on our enduring obsession with the phenomenon (and our enduring interest in casting it as something bad and bad for us or good and good for us) because of her ability to mesmerize a room and give pleasure by undressing.

One thing that is unique about the Houdini of Take Off is that she is a hybrid in American popular culture: a funny-smart sex symbol that became a star for mythic reasons and antimythic ones, too. Gypsy was the most eminent, sophisticated practitioner of what her producers labeled an "American" art. But she became an icon in large part because of one specific preposterous claim: she liked to read great books, listen to classical music, and take off her clothes onstage. This makes her a Confidence Girl, heir to American tricksters in Melville, Poe, and Twain. In *Huckleberry Finn* the Duke and the Dauphin pose as royalty and do a naked dance to defraud a man's heirs. When the family discovers the deceit, the pair get tarred and feathered. Arguments about whether Gypsy was really smart or not became arguments about what it meant to be American and what Making It cost women.

The Art of the Tease is divided into five sections. The book is chronological. I start with the real Gypsy and her family. Chapter Two records her arrival in New York and her efforts to forge a new identity. Chapter Three describes her botched trip to Hollywood and her return to New York. Chapter Four spans the forties and recounts how "The Queen of Striptease" transformed herself into "The Striptease Intellectual," and the backlash against her. This chapter is the largest part of the book, and it tells of the entertainment world's changing demands and of Gypsy's affinity with twentieth century American writers and artists. Chapter Five traces Gypsy's use of striptease to sell products including sheets, furs, and liquor. This section contains an analysis of the eponymous 1959 musical, and of the memoirs— her own, her son's, her sister's—which retold her story from their perspectives. I cannot think of another American family that has produced so many memoirs. I end with a brief description of an HBO movie currently in production about Gypsy, starring Sigourney Weaver.

Before modern pornography's rise, Gypsy moved the phenomenon of taking it off from America's margins to Broadway, Hollywood, and Main Street. For that Sisyphean task, she should get her own plaque in Union Square in New York City or a G-string in the striptease hall of fame.

ONE

Undressing the Family Romance

To Broadway aficionados, the name Gypsy Rose Lee recalls the 1959 eponymous musical (based on her memoir) created by Arthur Laurents, Stephen Sondheim, Jule Styne, and Jerome Robbins. These men saw Gypsy as a victim of Mama Rose, the stage-door mother who forced her daughter into a life of striptease. But the truth about Gypsy is more complicated than anything the musical or the memoir reveals. It is also more complicated than the three memoirs Gypsy's sister and son wrote about their extraordinary relative. No one could invent this woman who tore herself and her profession down at every opportunity. "The stage is 6 feet by 2 feet which is dandy for a coffin but not dandy for me," she complained about the San Francisco nightclub where she stripped in 1941.

If Gypsy was quick to deride the venues she played in, she was equally quick to apologize after putting on airs. In 1949 the Hollywood columnist Hedda Hopper published a catty remark Gypsy made about the lack of intelligence of a certain "Monkey Girl" in the carnival in which the stripper was then starring. The Monkey Girl writes an angry letter to Hopper, who forwards it to Gypsy. The stripper responded to her friend: "It makes me feel like a heel if I've really hurt her feelings. . . . She might have an M.A. for all I know."

The overall arc of Gypsy's life—the bare facts, as it were—is a first-class rags-to-riches story. But the closer you get to that life, the loopier the arc gets—it would have to, as her story itself is a tease. Even something as straightforward as Gypsy's birth date is uncertain. Some sources say that she was born Rose Louise Hovick in 1914, while others list 1911 as the year of her birth. In 1923 a Seattle doctor claimed that Mama Rose altered her birth certificate and that Gypsy was actually born in 1908. All stories about Gypsy's early life do agree that she spent her first years in Seattle in a family of domineering women who had meek or absent husbands, and that as a young child she toured on small-time vaudeville circuits in the West. She first stripped in 1929, endured vaudeville's death, burlesque's death, Hollywood's humiliation, the Depression, World War II, and television's rise. She produced a Broadway show, wrote two best-selling books (and two flops), toured with her own carnival show, and "retired" in 1959 to tend her garden. And host a TV show. And sell dog food.

Gypsy borrowed from Edith Wharton and Horatio Alger. She was self-made and aspirational. Her friend Janet Flanner once told her that her brilliance was to understand "as common sense what others regard as downright lunacy." Gypsy's younger sister, June Havoc, described her as having "a comic savagery in her manner." Carson McCullers, who met her in 1940, wrote that she was "witty, kind, very sensible, and utterly true to herself." Gypsy picked up these attributes from spending time alone in her childhood and from hanging around backstage since the age of four and watching her sister and others perform. And from performing herself. And, surely, here the consummate performer and monster whose alias is her mother deserves credit. Here are a few Dickensian tidbits about life with Mother: Rose declined to change her daughters' diapers between dusk and dawn; Rose told June that she tried to abort her; Rose made June "go on with the show" while she was sick with chicken pox and mumps. Later, when Rose pled poverty or cried illness it was prelude to a request for financial consolation. (It should be mentioned, however, that the above stories come from June's pen in her second memoir, in which the younger sister was playing one of her favorite games: "Let's even the score.")

In the stories about Mother that she began to publish in the mid-1940s, Gypsy tempers Rose's less savory qualities with a fierce maternal dedication. In one, later reprinted in her memoir, she recounts how, when she first started stripping in burlesque, other female performers began to receive poison pen letters. "Why don't you wise up and get out of the business?" one of these letters, signed "a well wisher," suggested. Unbeknownst to Louise, backstage Rose was stitching together her daughter's legend with these memos, as well as with large floral bouquets and mash notes "from an unknown admirer." When Rose noticed her daughter watching her she did not cringe in shame. "Get that ribbon and help me tie it around the handle," Rose commanded. And so at age fifteen Louise helped her mother invent her.

The Hovick Family Tree

Louise actually had already been rehearsing for that role for some time. But I tell this anecdote to suggest that the Hovicks were not the average American family of the time—or any time, for that matter. Rose was just one thorny branch in the Hovick matriarchy, where, as June put it, "men just didn't seem to last very long."

The Amazons liked to descend to comic flourishes. According to Gypsy's son, Erik Preminger, one of his mother's most menacing claims—about how her great-great-great-grandmother survived the Donner party by strapping human steaks around her torso—was a joke. "She always told that story with a laugh," he said. In America, devouring one's own offspring to survive is more than a joke, however. It is a way of forging your identity. Chez the Hovicks, it served as a motif—a badge of honor. Survival of the fittest was an inheritance whose principles could be passed down wherever you were—the frontier or showbiz or New York literary life.

But Gypsy's ancestors were restless. They came to Seattle from Minnesota in the early 1890s. Known as Big Lady, Gypsy's maternal grandmother, Anna, a traveling milliner/corset maker/con artist, sometimes lived in Seattle with her husband, Charlie Thompson, who worked for the Great Northern Expressway, the tramline connecting Chicago to the Pacific Northwest. But other times she traveled solo to San Francisco, Alaska, or Nevada. These were regions of the country populated by miners and prostitutes and so were not known for their politesse or family values. Big Lady sold women of easy virtue and saloon dancers embroidered lingerie, hats, and other baubles in person and by mail, although she neglected to tell potential buyers that they were participating in an auction and the woman who paid most for supplies would win the garment that she thought she already owned. Anna had four children. The traveling saleswoman taught her daughter, Rose, some tricks, but otherwise neglected her.

Two of the four Thompson children died young. Hurd, the boy, drowned in the summer of 1897 in Lake Union, near the family's house. (Years later, according to June, Mina, Rose's sister, then a young woman, would overdose.) A search party found Hurd's naked body under a log in the middle of the lake. Also according to June, after Hurd's death Big Lady put Rose in a convent to protect her. But in 1910 she married Jack Hovick, a reporter and newspaper advertising salesman of Norwegian descent who was also brother-in-law of *Seattle Times* business editor Fred Hammons. The Hovicks settled in West Seattle, an area west of the Puget Sound that Seattle had annexed in 1903. For a few years the family moved from one house to another and Jack Hovick changed jobs nearly as often: one year he was selling newspaper ads, the next year it was real estate ads.

Rose herself was no finalist for Parent of the Year. Gypsy was born in a blizzard in a roofless house with no running water. The newborn weighed twelve pounds. "The midwife picked you up . . . and washed you with snow," Rose told her daughter later. You don't have to be a Freudian to imagine that that moment might inform Gypsy's adult iciness. Around 1916 Rose, Jack, and Louise moved to Vancouver, where June was born. Rose and Jack divorced and Rose and the girls returned to Seattle the following year. They stayed briefly with Rose's father, and then they hit the road. Rose would remarry three more times, although none of the husbands stuck as much as her notion—which was in her blood and reinforced by movie magazines—that the family was going to be famous.

Rose was not the only American housewife enamored of show-biz. In the silent film and vaudeville era women all over the country were deserting their husbands and hitting the road in search of glamour and freedom. Early on it became clear that June, Louise's cute, talented, younger, and blonder sister, could toe dance. Rose called June's first stage act "Baby June," but renamed it "Dainty June" after June's baby teeth grew in. As late as 1926 theaters conflated the two acts, sometimes billing her as "Dainty Baby June," although by that time the star could not be called a baby. (June refers to herself by that name long after she had stopped touring.)

By our standards, there is something grotesque—even pornographic—about June's acts, but they were typical of the time. Wearing a thigh-length frilly dress and white kneesocks, June stood on her toes and sang sentimental or risqué songs. She auditioned for the Russian ballerina Anna Pavlova but failed to make much of an impression. In Hollywood, film producer Hal Roach cast June in bit parts. According to June, Roach was not interested in her Dainty act at all. He wanted her to play a street urchin in Harold Lloyd comedies like *Hey There!* After Hollywood, Baby June and company toured on the Orpheum Circuit, a string of vaudeville theaters in larger western towns. The less dainty June became, the more people Rose added to the act so that, by the early 1920s, they were traveling in a pack and billing themselves as "Dainty June and Her Newsboy Songsters."

Louise had remained home with Rose's father until age seven, when she joined her mother and sister. Like June, in one of her

Gypsy Rose Lee as a child, ca. 1922. Billy Rose Theatre Division,
The New York Public Library for the Performing Arts, Astor,
Lenox and Tilden Foundations

first numbers, "Hard Boiled Rose," she played a bad-girl that, despite the era's Victorianism, was de rigueur. A photo of Louise doing this number shows an ugly duckling who, even at this age, interested herself in undressing for the camera.

"Plug," as she was called, wears a feathered hat, a short-sleeved turtleneck, and white gloves. Arms akimbo, one leg cocked so that it sticks out of a slit in a skin-tight skirt, Plug is sneering. A girl who strips cannot be nice. A stage direction on the sheet music for "Hard Boiled Rose" instructs, "Pull skirt up." And she does. Louise also played "The Living Doll," or "the Mechanical Doll," a modern-day Coppelia who danced across the stage as though on an assembly line. Offstage, while June sported peroxide ringlets, a white (often dirty) rabbit fur coat, and full makeup. Louise wore knickers and a boy's cap and coat.

The life of the traveling vaudeville troupe was not easy. Dainty Baby June and company played all sorts of theaters, mob-run nightclubs, Shriner halls, and other B, C, and D list venues. They stole blankets and silverware from hotels. They slept in their car. In 1923, when child labor authorities seized Louise and June in Rochester, Rose telegrammed her father to wire good references from Seattle so she could get the girls back. During flush periods the family played in bigger theaters, where they met the stars of the day, like Eva Tanguay, the "I Don't Care" Girl, whose human firecracker act announced her indifference to the status quo. Perhaps this indifference impressed Louise, if her mother's had not already.

Fat enough as a teenager to be called "The Duchess," Louise did a walk-on appearance opposite Fanny Brice, by then a comic star. In her memoir Gypsy played down this meeting's importance, asking, "How could I learn anything when I was just atmosphere?" But to be "just atmosphere" is exactly the skill that Louise mastered, later modulating it the way people used to adjust the volume on the radio: by twirling.

During her adolescence, Louise discovered what would later become her trademark: books. Stories of how much and what she read would later provide much material for the press. But in 1924 Rose hired a tutor for the girls, one Olive Thompson (Gypsy calls her "Tompkins" in her memoir lest readers conclude that the two Thompsons were related). According to June, her sister not only remembered every one of the five classes they attended as children, she read *The Decameron* and Rabelais on her own. (It is hard to imagine better training for the Striptease Intellectual.) Gypsy's son Erik attributes a highbrow reading list to his mother: "Brontë and Browning, George Sand and Lytton Strachey." *Gypsy*, Gypsy's memoir, strikes a more credible note by focusing less on specific titles than on Louise's love of books and the people who read them. Escaping her mother and the theater in Detroit, at age fourteen Louise found herself in a bookstore-cafe managed by the young George Davis, whom she would meet again in New York in the 1940s. About the readers she saw she wrote: "They were all talking about books and their authors."

By her own account, the young burlesque comedian already loved to read. "My books had already broken the bottom out of the trunk June and I shared for our toys," she wrote. In this story, books are important not just for their own merits, but because they can help you reinvent yourself. When Louise stands in front of a copy of *Marius the Epicurean*, Davis steers her to Shakespeare's sonnets. Gypsy buys the sonnets, sneaks off to a corner of the hotel, and, in a prelude to one adult self, tries to write a play. But the author/star gets only as far as "I enter" before she wads up the paper and throws it in the trash. Still, though she has momentarily abandoned her literary career, Louise grasps books' other function. When, a little while later, Stanley, a newsboy in the act, hit on her, she asked, "Do you like to read?" and quoted from one of the sonnets. He kissed her.

By the age of fifteen, Louise had cycled through more roles than some people play in a lifetime: Hard Boiled Rose; Plug; the Duchess; Living Doll; intellectual; playwright; and ingénue. Later, when she reprised these roles, she seemed like a pro.

What's in a Name?

June eloped with one of the newsboys around the time vaudeville died. The Hovicks ate dog food, lived in a tent at the town dump, and pawned their belongings. But from deprivation came invention. Louise renamed the troupe "Louise and Her Hollywood Blondes" and made herself the star. Rose anted with "Rose Louise and Her Hollywood Blondes," the banner under which Gypsy would tour until she went solo in 1930.

According to *Gypsy*, the next chapter occurs when Louise was about to do her first striptease in burlesque. The star of "Rose Louise and Her Hollywood Blondes" renamed herself "Gypsy Rose Lee," hanging onto "Rose" as a remembrance of thorns, just as Erik would later keep "Lee" as a reminder that he was related to his mother by bile and betterment alike. The etymology of Gypsy Rose Lee is more than a hit parade of childhood resentments, however. Gypsy's memoir places her christening at the Gaiety Theatre in Toledo, the night of her first striptease. Gypsy writes that she chooses her name for the most ordinary of reasons: as an alias. She wanted to hide her new career from her grandfather. But if the name is a disguise, it is also her destination. She sensed that striptease belonged to her. "I knew that everyone was going to hear about us," she wrote.

In that era, the practice of women renaming themselves on Broadway and in Hollywood was hardly uncommon. Theodosia Goodman became Theda Bara. Mary Pickford was born Gladys Smith. But "Gypsy" conjured unique properties. A gypsy is also a fortune-teller, a reader of tea leaves, which Gypsy became, and the name also implies all varieties of impermanence, including the most literal one. For the rest of her life, Gypsy would always be moving. She chose a popular entertainer's lonely, peripatetic life over any other. "We're usually on the road," she lamented— or bragged—in 1957, reeling off the places she and her son Erik had touched down at Christmas in the past decade.

Gypsy was also a vagabond in terms of where she belonged: to showbiz? To the literati? To her mother? To burlesque? To what we would now call the sex industry? While Gypsy's rootlessness helped her crossover appeal, it also predicted that she would, like most famous female celebrities of her era, wind up alone. The name Gypsy took reflected this irony. But it also distinguished itself by simple elegance at a time when other strippers called themselves by their given names or took showy monikers like "the Golden Girl." Then there is the Freudian point of view: "Gypsy Rose Lee" achieves its aura by stitching together bits of Gypsy's past in ways that expose its holder's unconscious. Rose, which is feminine and a flower, doubles as her mother's name and hers—Gypsy might as well have called herself "Gypsy My Mother Myself Lee." Lee, like Louise, begins with "L," plus it adds a homespun quality to Gypsy Rose that would have enhanced her appeal to the working-class burlesque audience of that era. If you subtract her last name, the phrase "Gypsy Rose" suggests her material ascent. (Later in life Gypsy would sign letters "Gypola," which sounds more like a product than a person, as well as a 1950s-style con.) Gypsy used names to separate herself from her family in other ways, too. According to one story, she dropped "Hovick" because the public confused it with "Havoc," the name her sister took.

Twice in her life American puritanism forced Gypsy to revert to her given name, Louise Hovick, to hide her burlesque past. This was not simply an inconvenience or a career setback. The second time, in 1937 in Hollywood, "was absolute misery," she confessed in a letter to her friend Hedda Hopper, as though being denied her name erased the self she had worked so hard to build and left her with a stranger.

Gypsy Reinvents Striptease: Burlesque and Illusion, 1927–29

When Gypsy first took off her clothes onstage, striptease had only been around for a year or two. The woman formerly known as Rose Louise Hovick was as prescient as those nerds who became Silicon Valley millionaires before anyone knew about the Internet. Or to understand the significance of Gypsy's undertaking, one could go back to the early Jazz Age, when the Algonquin Round Table and other intellectuals "discovered" burlesque. Celebrated by Edmund Wilson in the pages of the *New Republic* or by Hart Crane in *The Bridge*, or by e.e. cummings or anyone in the *New Yorker*, burlesque (the lowest form of entertainment) in the 1920s had two things going for it: half-dressed women dancing and comics wearing enormous rubber phalluses. Burlesque made sex real and funny. "Burlesque . . . centered," wrote Douglas Gilbert in his history of vaudeville, "about the apertures of the human body."

In the 1920s, too much of an aperture was a good thing. Burlesque's savaging of high culture and Victorian ideas about sex inspired the Timothy Greenfield-Sanderses of their day to invent populist slogans about democratic ideals in entertainment—"the poor man has a right to depravity as much as the rich." But these slogans also indicate how seriously intellectuals took burlesque: they considered it a popular form of entertainment that was as vital as the circus, comic books, and silent films.

Striptease became burlesque's main event the same year as talkies were born. The love affair soured, and burlesque impresarios doubled the number of shows and performers. Three striptease shows a day was the downside of Taylorism. Intellectuals wondered: could women taking off their clothes on an "assembly line" truly count as popular entertainment? It was odd enough that a white Jewish comedian in blackface singing "Mammy" decimated silent film. But odder still that whereas in Hollywood the talkies made silent film actors irrelevant, in New York the strippers made burlesque comedy obsolete by adding their undressing, shimmying bodies.

Burlesque theaters were not our nation's most glamorous spaces. In her description of the backstage at the Missouri Theatre—the Kansas City theater where, according to her memoir, she acted in her first burlesque scene in 1927—Gypsy wrote:

"Cigarette butts and empty coffee containers and old newspapers were all kicked together with dirty frayed satin shoes under the make up shelf. Gnats swarmed around a half empty container of beer resting on the edge of a filthy sink that was filled with laundry left overnight to soak. Sticky red lip rouge smudges encircled the top of the container. Under each lip-rouge smudge, penciled in with eyebrow pencil, was an initial. The mirrors were broken. Their jagged edges reached out like claws. Shreds of net and bits of rhinestone and beads hung by thin strings on nails behind mirrors."

The film close-up showed Americans actors' and especially actresses' faces in greater detail than ever before, but in burlesque women stripped on a runway just above the audience—a corporeal rendering of the blown-up faces the camera displayed. If you reached out you could touch the performers. The male comics played scenes far away on the proscenium stage as if to announce their irrelevance. But burlesque did not exactly deliver what it advertised. Gypsy's first burlesque scene was called "Illusion." Her punch line, "I'm no illusion. I'm real—Here, take my hand—touch me. Feel me," anticipates the quality that she would spend her life developing. More skeptical minds called her illusion a gimmick, a word that had entered the American vocabulary a few years earlier.

The first striptease. Billy Rose Theatre Division, The New York Public Library for the Performing Arts, Astor, Lenox and Tilden Foundations

In Gypsy's memoir, the story of her first striptease conflates several stories from showbiz mythology. One concerns the adage "the show must go on." In that myth's burlesque version, Ed Ryan, the producer of "Girls from the Follies," had hired blonde-haired Gladys Clark, who doubled as a stripper and a musician who could play both the accordion and the clarinet. But Clark went on a bender and disappeared. A star was born. Another myth asserts that striptease appeared in the hinterlands like soybeans or corn. According to Gypsy's memoir, she first took it off neither in Paris nor in New York; the location of her inaugural act was either Toledo, Ohio, in the fall of 1929, or just after the New Year of 1930 in Kansas City.

As for why she did it, the musical turns Gypsy into a victim: Rose Louise Hovick is a girl whose mother pimps her into a life of taking off her clothes onstage. Yet in her memoir Gypsy does not protest when Rose suggests that she strip. Was she an exhibitionist or a patsy? How much of the striptease was the result of Gypsy's desire to strip, and how much of it was the result of her mother's urging? It is impossible to know. Gypsy contributed to the "my mother made me do it" theory of striptease in her memoir but also suggested that she liked to undress in public. What is known is that, in the mid-1930s, Gypsy began telling a story about her first striptease—contradicted by the photo of her childhood mugging—that refers to it as an accident. This recycles yet another showbiz myth. Stories about striptease's invention almost always involve the performer standing onstage, caught in the spotlight, her strap slipping from her shoulder. Only when the crowd goes wild does she take off the other strap. The idea of a woman stripping of her own accord is too naughty—the shy creature is reluctant to take off her clothes, until her audience draws her in. She is, in the vulgar phrase, giving the people what they want.

But although Gypsy absorbed these earlier ideas, her story about her first striptease distinguishes itself from the more conventional ones. For one, it emphasizes self-invention. From the start Gypsy designed and sewed her own strip gowns, signaling that she was fashioning her own identity out of tulle and spangles and not accepting one that someone else made for her. The second unique aspect of her story is modesty. By the standards of the day, Gypsy's first costumes were virginal. In one she stripped to "ten yards of lavender net and three bunches of violets sewn on a flesh colored leotard." The costume she wore in her second-act number in Toledo was a full-length gown made of red velvet. With it she wore the kind of red picture hat that Vivien Leigh would later don. She would hide behind the hat for the encore, in a teddy or a bodysuit or a one-piece bathing suit with lacing up the side.

During this era Gypsy made unfinished seams a part of her act. The dressmakers' pins holding together her outfit wound up in the orchestra pit, as if to comment on her own incompleteness. Also, she may have been the first stripper to wear a bridal gown onstage.

Even from this early point, Gypsy brings the con in striptease to the surface. When you go to see a striptease, you are going with the understanding that you will see someone take off their clothes, that it will be sexy, that it will titillate. Gypsy was never much interested in this as a goal. She was promising sex but she was delivering its illusion, playing three-card monte with her audience's desire. She was asking a metaphysical question: What is left when we reveal everything? But she was also laughing. To strip as a bride parodies marriage; to ask all of these highfalutin questions while throwing your garter into the audience parodies the sanctity of matrimony.

Gypsy thought of her striptease as sleight-of-hand. More than anyone else on the scene, she stripped as though the world had drained her of heat and inflated her with whatever force animated "the mechanical doll."

Gypsy's striptease coincided with the worst economic crisis in American history. The connection between one woman undressing and the Great Depression, however farfetched it seems, may explain why the few publicity photos of Gypsy from 1929 evoked tragedy. At first I thought that the artificial teardrops on Gypsy's cheeks in these sepia close-ups signified melancholy, or perhaps talent, since to cry, being a sign of good acting, could redeem the stripper from the purgatory of being unable to sing or dance. But then I understood: she was crying to express remorse for her role in the nation's economic woes.

TWO

The Queen of Striptease

As the Depression settled over the country, Gypsy performed in burlesque theaters across America, from Chicago to St. Louis, from Washington to Newark. By the time she arrived in New York at the end of 1930, she had dropped her supporting cast the way other strippers dropped their garters onstage.

If striptease started in the Midwest, New York—which is always about the solo act—made taking off your clothes a sophisticated one-woman spectacle. There is something poignant about New York burlesque creating the lone stripper in an era of socialist fervor. The vulnerable undressing woman onstage mirrored the Depression era American audience in the dark theater; both watcher and watched sat isolated by solitude and hunger. The lone stripper gyrated across the stage and up and down the runway, so near though untouchable, jerking her way through her halfhearted orgiastic dances. And yet few observers saw it that way.

New York was several years away from electing as mayor Fiorello La Guardia, who made cleaning up burlesque and striptease one of his most vociferous crusades. To describe burlesque before La Guardia is like evoking the Garden of Eden before the Fall. And yet La Guardia's crusade also made strippers suddenly aware of their own economic worth. In the early years of the Depression, New York politicians and reformers had only just begun to figure out that targeting the Minsky brothers—the most notorious burlesque theater owners in the city—as evidence of the era's depravity might distract Americans from their economic pain. So when Billy Minsky, the brains behind his family's success, saw the overdressed Gypsy (billed in Newark, New Jersey, as "Gypsy" Rose Lee), he might have hoped that she would stave off reformers by way of a practical joke. Who would arrest an overdressed stripper?

By then Minsky had exhausted his repertoire of jokes/gestures—wearing top hats, advertising in the *New Yorker*, costuming ushers in French maid outfits. Looking for a funny way to deflect city officials' charges that his family was the city's first flesh mongers, he advised Gypsy to straighten her hair to be "more ladylike." She complied. For the rest of her career she wore her hair off her face in an elaborate upsweep—what one critic later described as the style of "the divine Sarah"—to emphasize restraint. The long, sultry locks of a Veronica Lake were not for her.

But while Gypsy posed as a Victorian stripper, the Minskys wanted audiences to see that her roots were in the Lower East Side. So, in April 1931, they gave her debut striptease at the Republic Theatre on Forty-second Street in a Yiddish inflection meant to make Depression era New Yorkers laugh. The Minskys titled the show that Gypsy starred in "Ada Onion from Bermuda" and advertised it with a phrase that mocked the tagline of the Ziegfeld Follies, New York's most respectable revue ("Glorified American Girls"): "Gypsie Rose Lee: The Most Beautiful Girl in the World." The *New York Evening Journal* wondered how "Ada Onion" would succeed given that she was "All Dressed Up for Burlesque?" But another paper asked: "She's like a breath of spring. How far would she go in show biz?"

Until Gypsy arrived, the question was moot, since no stripper had gone anywhere. Trade papers tended to describe certain numbers as being "almost" good enough for Broadway, but no stripper had made it to the Great White Way. The five burlesque theaters crammed on Forty-second Street between Eighth and Ninth Avenues (as well as those in Harlem and downtown) pulsed with Hollywood and Broadway wannabes, the B-girls and pinups of their day.

Burlesque strippers in these theaters did what *Variety* described as "sex showmanship," which, though the Minskys might have claimed it to be artistry, many Americans associated with obscenity. Strippers flashed G-strings or lay down on the stage and crossed and uncrossed their legs. They painted their bodies with radium. They did "marionette" strips, "bubble" strips, and "muff" strips. They named themselves "Peaches Strange" and "Dynamic Dolly." The stripper would bump and grind or, back to audiences, shake her behind or "quiver"; she would also do the "tassel twirl," spinning tiny pieces of fabric from her nipples in circles like airplane propellers. Only one other stripper of this era—Ann Corio—took it off coyly.

What did Gypsy's striptease circa 1931 look like? Decorum and the obfuscating Broadway slang of the day makes it difficult to re-create. But a few things about Gypsy's early numbers (she rotated them) are known. She sometimes stripped to Cab Calloway's "Minnie the Moocher," before Betty Boop made it her anthem. According to Martin Collyer, in "Seven Minutes of Sheer Art" Gypsy "kidded the lacy underpants off the more earnest of strippers." Gypsy did not strip to the altogether, at least not at Minsky's in 1931. When she was arrested at the Republic the morning after her premiere, telegrams offered to protect her as though she were a virgin in distress and not a loose woman. One tabloid quoted Gypsy as explaining that she made the detective wait outside while she dressed. Another claimed that she rode to the precinct in a limo. According to the *New York Evening Graphic*, the arrest raised her status. Gypsy received "six proposals of marriage, one live bunny, a dozen bouquets of American beauties, numberless boxes of candy, forty-four mash notes and a case of ginger ale."

"My baby is innocent and pure," Rose told the *New York Evening Graphic* when Gypsy made the cover in a body suit with flowers over her private parts. "I wasn't naked . . . I was completely covered by a blue spotlight," Gypsy said. "Just ask my mother, who is always with me." Gypsy was eventually cleared of all charges. The detectives who arrested her admitted that she had not flashed anything obscene. (Except for a mother-daughter love song that would never be heard again. According to Mort Minsky, his brother Billy had banned Rose from the Republic Theater early on, because, as he put it, "her river did not run to the sea.")

In the months that followed, Gypsy worked around town and toured with her old show, "Girls from the Follies." But Midwestern audiences scorned a stripper who took off only one or two garments. When "Follies" hit Chicago, *Variety* wrote: "Gypsy Rose Lea [*sic*] has no following locally for her disrobing talent and she's hardly likely to acquire one, since she impresses as being a sentimental, old-fashioned sort of a strip tease dancer." Back in New York, the "sentimental, old-fashioned" dancer bought her first house, in Rego Park, then part of Long Island. It was big enough for Rose and June.

While stripping for Minsky, Gypsy had befriended, or been

befriended by, bootlegger Waxy Gordon. It is not clear whether she was Gordon's lover or just "arm candy," but the two shared rags-to-riches stories later immortalized in Broadway musicals. As Albert Fried, a historian of gangsters, put it, although Gordon had started out as a thug in the Jazz Age, in the Depression "he was reborn Irving Wexler, free-spending New York business-man, owner of real estate and stocks and other properties of a vaguer nature . . . a gentleman about town conspicuous by his fancy dress and limousine and companions."

By 1932, it was hardly uncommon for gangsters to fund Broad-way shows and nightclubs. The Great White Way was a mess. None of the producers that had flourished in the Jazz Age had any money. Broke and ill with pneumonia, Florenz Ziegfeld, who had made his name in the 1920s with the beloved Follies revues, borrowed funds to produce his last original show, *Hot-Cha*, from Wexler and his colleague Dutch Schultz, the "King of Beer." The cast included Bert Lahr, sexy movie star Lupe Velez, dancers Yolanda and Velez, and Eleanor Powell. The artistic team com-prised Joseph Urban, Charles LeMaire, and Mark Hellinger. But *Hot-Cha* (whose subtitle, *Laid in Mexico*, was contributed by Wex-ler) is no Follies. The vacuous plot concerns a Brooklyn waiter (Lahr) who, on his Mexican vacation, gets transformed into a matador.

After Gypsy stripped in a benefit performance for Wexler, he paid for her dental work and introduced her to *Hot-Cha*'s songwriter, Lew Brown. Waiting in line at the audition, Gypsy made the acquaintance of the Titian-haired Hope Dare, the girlfriend of Dutch Schultz's lawyer, Richard Dixie Davis, whom she would later help hide upstate. The producers cast Gypsy in several minor roles, including "Girl in Compartment."

Gypsy failed to save the show. *Hot-Cha* ran for only fifteen weeks. The real drama was backstage. Even though the credits list Gypsy as "Rose Louise," the cast somehow learned of her Minsky's past. When *Hot-Cha* opened in February 1932 in Washington, D.C., the showgirls complained that they had to share a dressing room with a stripper until publicist Bernard Sobel saved Gypsy from this showbiz snobbery: "I fired my first shot by placing Gypsy's picture in every important paper in the capital," he recalled. When *Hot-Cha* arrived in New York the following month, Sobel continued playing White Knight. He got Gypsy invited to a party attended by John Farrar, the founder of Farrar and Rinehart and, later, Farrar, Straus, and Co., and his wife, Margaret, the syndicated crossword puzzle columnist. "The meal had scarcely begun when I noticed to my surprise that the conversation concerned books with Gypsy taking the lead," he wrote. Despite her literary savvy, Gypsy could not find work on Broadway.

Twelve months passed before George White cast Gypsy in his *Melody*, a romantic comedy with music by Sigmund Romberg and lyrics by Irving Caesar. Although White, a former dancer with the Ziegfeld Follies, had by that time garnered a following for the yearly revue he produced—George White's *Scandals—Melody* was not a hit. The fluffy, old-fashioned operetta spanning the years between 1880 and 1933 ran for about fifty performances at the Casino Theatre. Set in Paris, *Melody* begins as an aristocratic woman cuckolds her aristocratic husband with the composer she really loves. The plot then leaps forward to show that act's effect on the heroine's heirs. One critic called it "delightfully melodious." "Rose Louise" plays "Claire Lolive, Pierre's Mistress," in the first act. Years later Gypsy recalled how she interpolated her shtick into the nondescript role, crying "ouch" as, exiting, her bustle stuck in the door (playing this role may have given her the idea of starting her striptease numbers in Gay Nineties costumes). Although Bernard Sobel compared Gypsy's performance to that of the torch singer Helen Morgan (she sang one number), other critics panned her. "Gypsy Rose Lee's career has not been spectacular," wrote Irving Drutman in 1935.

But Gypsy nourished her own ideas about "spectacular": she wanted to use her Broadway persona uptown to inform her stripteases downtown, and vice versa. Some gave in to her charms, especially when doing so could tweak intellectuals. Recounting her activities, the *New York Times* observed: "Miss Lee panicked the guests by a cool appreciation of *The Good Earth*." (Pearl Buck's book had recently won the Pulitzer Prize.) Panicked? The only stripper to modify her sex appeal with a deadpan appreciation for culture, Gypsy figured out that Depression era Broadway and Hollywood were full of tough guys and acid-tongued girls who talked as though they had read Proust. A woman from nowhere could exceed these stars by adding striptease to the mix.

What about the private life of the young stripper on her way up? Common wisdom about Gypsy says that she was less interested in men than in money. Or that she was gay, which some sociologists in the 1960s insisted that strippers are supposed to be. But these opinions come from her family, or "experts," or people like Arthur Laurents—not the best sources of information on Gypsy's sexual taste. Although there was more to Gypsy's romantic life than noli me tangere, none of these labels describes her relationship with the opposite sex in the 1930s or in any other era.

"Our friend is much too pretty for me. I like my men on the monster side, a snarling mouth, evil eye, broken nose. If he should happen to have thick ears, good!" Gypsy writes to Charlotte Seitlin, Simon and Schuster publicity director in 1941, after hearing that a mutual acquaintance thought she was witty and wanted to marry her. Gypsy resisted dating men who would compete with her for center stage. Coming from a matriarchy, she may have been wary about binding herself to the opposite sex in general. And men may have been intimidated by her considerable earning power. In *More Havoc*, June recounts how Gypsy, newly arrived to New York, confided that she was going to have to rape someone to lose her virginity. This is one of the few moments where the truth of the younger sister's words overrides her bitterness and presents an American paradox: the woman who stripped for a living was a virgin. The great sex symbol was sexless.

Working in burlesque may have aggravated Gypsy's boy problem: although she came out of the era of the Stage Door Johnny, in burlesque the Johnnies, "less refined" than those who hung around Broadway theaters, could not catapult a girl to a better life. (Only one stripper married European royalty—Rozelle the Golden Girl.)

But in 1933 Gypsy began seeing a married socialite, "Eddy," whom the writer Laura Jacobs outs in a 2003 *Vanity Fair* profile as Eddy Braun. Eddy gave Gypsy a copy of *The Waves* as well as some Tiffany bracelets. Supposedly about to divorce his wife, the generous and handsome man inconveniently dropped dead. Gypsy took up with dental supplies salesman Bob Mizzy, whom Erik Preminger describes was Eddy's beard.

From Banned in Boston to Kicked Out of the Casino

Gypsy left town. That fall, at Minsky's in Boston, she stripped to "Minuet in G." Boston had long been more puritanical than New York, and Gypsy's act, titled "Burlesque Moderne," was notable for two reasons. First, a photographer at the *Boston Daily Record* shot Gypsy taking off her clothes and published the pictures, which attracted the Watch and Ward Society, Boston's censor. The *Record* called her a star and the society's director denounced her just as he had denounced Aldous Huxley, Erich Maria Remarque, H. L. Mencken, Herbert Asbury, and Voltaire. Second, the *Harvard Lampoon* devoted a page to Gypsy, demonstrating her appeal to the Ivy League.

The heroine and sinner returned to New York and worked briefly at the Casino de Paree, the gangster-funded cavernous nightclub-sideshow-theater on Fifty-second Street. Launched by the impresario Billy Rose, this club aimed to get around censorship laws by providing "family entertainment." Gypsy emceed there until she incorrectly introduced the vaudeville team Gomez and Winona. According to Gypsy's account, she looked at Fanny Brice—then Rose's wife—at that moment and, hoping that Brice would remember her, jumbled the team's names. Afterward, Billy Rose fired her. But according to Rose, he fired Gypsy after she refused to pose naked for him. Rose was outraged that his former employee explained her decision financially as opposed to morally: she made five times as much stripping downtown at the Irving Place Burlesque theatre as she made at his nightclub, she said. Either way, getting kicked out of Boston and fired from the Casino de Paree helped transform a demure stripper into the Queen of Striptease.

1934–35: "A Princess Takes Off Her Pants"

Gypsy used her burlesque money to buy distance between her and Rose and, in the summer of 1934, she moved downtown to an apartment on Gramercy Park. With plans to entertain, she placed a chrome bar in the drawing room's center and a small piano in the corner. Meanwhile, Gypsy installed Rose uptown in a nine-room apartment on Riverside Drive. According to June, Rose—who is generally assumed to have been gay—opened a lesbian "boardinghouse" and served moonshine, stag movies, and spaghetti on Tuesday and Friday evenings. But uptown wasn't far enough away.

That same year the stripper bought Rose a two-story brown colonial mansion in Highland Mills, an hour north of New York. The press gave Gypsy's acquisition of this house more coverage than it did her purchase of the one in Rego Park a few years earlier. And for good reason. Witchwood Manor boasted a steeply angled roof, five bathrooms, a stone fireplace, and a huge library with built-in bookcases that she filled with books. Signed photographs of celebrities hung on the mantel. Gypsy had decorated the seats of the dining room chairs with her own needlepoint designs, and in the basement she had built a small theater complete with a lighting board. She stored the life-size lobby cut-outs of herself there, too. When important guests arrived at her Gramercy Park penthouse she shoved her mother out the servant's entrance and sent her back to the Upper West

Side or upstate, away from the icon she was transforming her-self into.

In 1934, the Irving Place released the huckster in Gypsy, the bunco artist, the shyster, the inauthentic. Or that is how many Americans would have seen it. In this light, Gypsy's talent becomes facile, and even suspect, as opposed to the honestly won attributes we like to consider natural to American women. For example, her campaign to make striptease respectable, if you want to call it that, which really revs up here, recalls P. T. Barnum's mid-nineteenth century attempts to convince Americans that a stuffed monkey was the "FeeJee mermaid" and that viewing this monkey was educational. Like Barnum, Gypsy's Ripley's Strip-It-or-Not act titillated and angered Americans.

But Gypsy's act brings out something else that I would call courage. I do not put her in the same rank as Elizabeth Cady Stanton, nor is she a feminist in the first-wave sense of the word, although to my mind she anticipates Gloria Steinem. At the Irving Place, Gypsy created a sexy, smart persona to protest both burlesque's crassness and puritanism's mean-spiritedness. She is more Sister Carrie than Carrie Bradshaw. In the 1920s many striptease acts looked like melodrama or tragedy. The character of the vamp flung herself about the stage undressing or lurked, like a spider, to trap her male victim. Jazz Age stripteasers played the fly in "spider and fly" numbers literalizing the vamp's situation, or virgin maids caught in the act of striptease "unawares." In a photo from 1929 Gypsy poses as one of these vamps, in chains. But besides that she rarely borrowed from female entertainers of an earlier generation who sang melancholy songs about their men or did Apache dances in which at the finale the male partner knocked them out to punish them for expressing their sexuality.

At the Irving Place Gypsy's numbers (performed solo) were elegant and comic, or simply comic. Some were downright goofy. One was a "reverse" striptease in which she took off her undergarments but kept on her dress, dramatizing the principle that, in striptease, what lay beneath was more exciting. In other numbers Gypsy disabused her audiences of the notion, handed down from fin-de-siècle France, of the "accidental" striptease, which titillated along the lines of the peep show. Although you were in a theater, if you suspended disbelief, you happened upon Yvette "going to bed" or Celine "finding" a flea in her lingerie. Gypsy's approach made striptease American, intentional, and friendly. At a time when couples dancing was in vogue, Gypsy remained still or paraded regally across the stage.

Gypsy was able to enact these dramas at the Irving Place Burlesque Theatre, located off of Irving Place, in part because producer Allan Gilbert aspired to be the Billy Minsky of Fifteenth Street. Not much is known about the fellow who promoted Gypsy as his number one stripper.

In one solo, when Gypsy sashayed onstage wearing long white opera gloves and a tight red velvet dress that flared at the hips, her walk—the so-called parade up and down the stage—was devastating. Even more devastating was the moment when she broke the languorous pace to rip off her "breakaway" dress—as dresses with removable panels were called—with startling rapidity.

In Gypsy's most written-about and enduring striptease from this era, she wears a polka-dotted blouse and long, black taffeta skirt as though she were a Sunday School teacher circa 1890. Gypsy ended this number in a distinctly un-schoolteacher way, flashing polka-dotted bows on her breasts. The number, which lasted for a record-breaking ten minutes, included an encore in which Gypsy, peeping from behind the stage curtain, dangled her garter in front of the audience the way a man might dangle a bone in front of a dog. Gypsy inverted the peep show—she was peeping at the peepers. Also during this period Gypsy transformed the act of throwing pins into the audience into a metaphor about the sexes. Tossing her petticoat over the tuba player's head (or sometimes into the tuba)—as if giving a man femininity's accoutrements—she could make the audience laugh at striptease's come-hither-do-not-touch-me attitude.

By 1933 the audience needed that laugh, even if it came out as a choke. At the Depression's nadir, the unemployment rate had soared to nearly 25 percent nationwide, and breadlines, soup kitchens, and shantytowns were everywhere. Americans sought refuge in burlesque theaters; the pin dropping and petticoat tossing might distract them momentarily from their hunger. (Always looking for a way to raise the stakes, Gypsy later determined that the audience could redeem the pins at the box office for a free show.)

After the New Deal began to stabilize the economy, Gypsy widened the gap between herself and all other strippers by immersing herself further in the past. She eschewed the lingua franca of striptease—the bump and grind—the weaving of the hips that would, in a year or two, contribute to politicians' opinion that burlesque was driving the wave of sex crimes sweeping the city. Gypsy's immobility made her less threatening and even suggested the *tableaux vivantes* of the 1890s or the betighted burlesque troupes of the 1860s rather than the strippers who, elsewhere, the tabloids reported, sometimes "forgot" to wear their G-strings. At a moment when Fred Astaire and Ginger Rogers were gliding together through space, Gypsy stood still, alone on stage, reciting her lyrics like a schoolgirl at a poetry competition. Gypsy likewise rejected the zipper—only then coming into wide usage in women's clothing. Whereas stripping by unzipping was thought to encourage sexual intimacy, using pins allied Gypsy with a more modest era and canceled out—or tried to cancel out—her stripping in the first place.

Critics often ridiculed strippers for not being able to dance or sing. Gypsy boasted that she became a stripper *because* she could do neither—a good example of how she used misdirection to distract her audience. But her most consequential innovation is that she talked while disrobing. This era's burlesque made only one other role available to women besides stripping: "The Talking Woman," a phrase that sounds odd to our ears since it can suggest that strippers, by not speaking, lack "a voice," to use the modern feminist description. Gypsy's patter distracted from her pageant of undressing, as it confused categories and made her a modern funny girl.

Still more outrageous, Gypsy's performing voice—and recordings exist from radio, television, and LPs such as the 1962 *Gypsy Rose Lee Remembers Burlesque* or the 1958 *That's Me All Over*—did not use Brooklynese street-smart language; she spoke in rounded Mid-Atlantic tones, sprinkling French phrases and *mots justes* throughout. Gypsy would also pair ingenuous, cloying sentimental lyrics with her striptease. For example, here is the first stanza of her number "I'm a Lonesome Little Eve":

I'm a lonesome little Eve
Looking for an Adam
Gee I wish I had him,
Cuddling me, 'neath the shade of the tree

And in our garden we would be so happy
I'm a lonesome little Eve
All I do is sit and grieve

Munching an apple, Gypsy would mince down the circular staircase the Irving Place Theatre had installed after the License Commissioner had outlawed its runway. She would toss the core to the audience, where she had arranged for a shill to fall out of his box while grabbing for it. A spotlight caught his pratfall. And suddenly "Lonesome Little Eve" becomes a man-eating heroine who strips the apple eater of his humanity and exposes him as a pervert.

In her take on the 1930s brutality between men and women, Gypsy's numbers sometimes recall Mae West and Jean Harlow in their most ferocious screen roles. She took "Powder My Back," which she stole from an unknown ingénue in 1929, and stretched it into a Thurberesque battle of the sexes. Armed with a powder puff on a long stick, she wandered up and down the runway, inviting customers to powder her back "every morn." But this was no scented invitation to the boudoir. As in "Lonesome Little Eve," she seemed to avenge herself against the men who powdered too hard (even if accidentally). She pranced down the aisle and kissed the "bald heads," leaving a lipstick imprint and braided comb-overs on their scalps. The joke was on them. Gypsy's striptease numbers—even the ones in which she stripped to the waist or leapt onto customers' laps—toyed with these contrasts in one way or another.

For all the Minskys' aspirational stunts, the Republic had only ever attracted theater columnists. By contrast, the Irving Place drew American writers, who found in burlesque a squalid authenticity. Writers' interest in these theaters goes beyond the adage that sex sells; they were seeking literary realism and a new way to explain the swirling action and the happy-unhappy relations between men and women in 1930s New York. Among the most famous writers in this category was Henry Miller, who described Gypsy in March 1935 at a Sunday matinee at the Irving Place Theatre, where she was starring in "Give Me a Lay": "She had a Hawaiian lei in her hand and she was telling how it felt to get a good lay, how even mother would be grateful for a lay once in a while. She said she'd take a lay on the piano, or on the floor. An old-fashioned lay, too, if needs be." I am a little suspicious of Gypsy's "Hawaiian" period, as no other account of it appears. But more important, Miller's blasé reaction to Gypsy's candor—her brand of frank sexual revelation was hardly the norm in 1935—indicates that he had spent too much time in Paris with Anaïs Nin.

Miller went on to the other performers. "In the first half hour everyone moves down to the good seats in the front. The strippers talk to their customers as they do their stunt. The coup de grace comes when they having divested themselves of every inch of clothing, there is only a spangled girdle with a fig leaf in front, sometimes a little monkey beard, which is quite ravishing. As they draw towards the wings, they stick their bottoms out and slip the girdle off. Sometimes they darken the stage and give a belly dance in radium paint. It's good to see their bellies glowing in the dark or them holding their boobies, especially when said boobies are full of milk."

Other writers played Margaret Mead (*Coming of Age in Samoa* had been published a few years earlier) and wrote about Gypsy as an urban primitive with some of the condescension implied by such an approach. *New Yorker* contributor and *World Telegram* newsman Joseph Mitchell went into the heart of burlesque darkness and came back with a story about a piece of the real New York few people had visited. In his 1936 collection of essays from the *New York Herald-Tribune*, titled *My Ears Are Bent*, he wrote, "Gypsy Rose Lee . . . is fond of working with a lot of clothes. At the Irving Place, she used to come out dressed in a big white fur coat. She would glide languidly across the stage, a sort of bound-for-the-opera walk. On her way back into the wings she would twitch the coat open with a negligent gesture, and the customers would go crazy, the bums." Mitchell's use of the past indicative allows him to distinguish himself from "the bums" more than Miller's present tense. But journalists were not the only ones watching. In a 1942 letter to Gypsy, the critic Carl van Doren recalled that at the Irving Place she was an American original, "a princess taking off her pants."

No female writer regarded Gypsy as a worthy subject, and it is hard not to wonder what Gertrude Stein or Anaïs Nin or even Dorothy Parker or Anita Loos would say about the Queen of Burlesque. The first women to mention Gypsy in print, the gossip columnists of the 1940s, did so in the spirit of promotion, not criticism. Women writers' silence continued. Where is Simone de Beauvoir or Germaine Greer on striptease? But these questions raise another one: what would the writing about Gypsy be like if she stripped today, when taking it off is so much more a phenomenon by, for, and of women than it used to be?

In the spring of 1935 Gypsy took up with Rags Ragland, a brilliant alcoholic burlesque comic, former truck driver, and boxer whom she had first met at Minsky's. A few years earlier, Ragland, who would die of uremia at age forty in 1946, was romantic and fun. He sent Gypsy rhyming kiddie-grams. "I would like to kiss you if I could because you have been so very good." No matter how hard Gypsy tried to edit Ragland out of the picture, he remained in the frame. That spring, when she was admitted to the PolyClinic Hospital for what Ragland called a "bum uterus," he sent her a love letter from Baltimore, which began with rows of kisses and included the promise that, if she didn't write him, "I'll have to come back there and pick you up and take you up some dark alley and give you the old razzle dazzle."

Later, Gypsy would try to capture Rags's mischievous voice and style in her plays.

Highbrow magazines continued to profess confusion as to how Gypsy became a star. As the "Talk of the Town" section of the *New Yorker* put it in June of 1935, "all she did was off her clothes." It was, the magazine concluded in a not altogether satisfying or satisfied way, the way that she did it. Even the *New Yorker* had to admit that there was no method for quantifying striptease or explaining how its allure worked, what made one woman better than another. There was no language to describe it without resorting to either euphemism or obscenity.

But the Irving Place became more than just a laboratory where Gypsy worked out undressing's physical properties—let's call her efforts the theory of relative striptease. The Irving Place was also the crucible where Gypsy's political conscience was born. It would be easy to dismiss this conscience as silly. If you are enamored of the left-leaning 1930s you could mistake Gypsy for an antecedent of the American celebrities flirting with Kabbalah and Iraq today. Gypsy did flirt. But she also deflated Socialist pieties as energetically as she deflated conventional attitudes toward sex. Communists, who noticed her wearing her mink coat over her strip gown as she passed through Union Square on her way from her Gramercy Park apartment to the theater, mistook her for a doyenne and heckled her. She responded: taking off her clothes five times a day on stage was more work than squawking political slogans from a soapbox.

Beneath her "I'm more proletarian than you" pose, Gypsy harbored a more serious political commitment. As one of the few female members of the short-lived burlesque union, the Burlesque Artists' Association, she participated in a three-day strike in September of 1935 that closed the theaters. Newspapers put her picture in the paper. But she was not just a figurehead. When Minsky's locked out the stagehands, the former stripper Red Tova Halem recalled: "Gypsy called our theater and asked for some pickets. All of us strippers put robes on over our G-strings" and "paraded outside the theater flashing passersby and shouting 'Don't go in there, boys.'" The Minskys settled with the stagehands that night.

Never one to romanticize her sister's beginnings, June saw the Irving Place less as a worker's paradise than as what used to be called a "blue theater." The younger sister asked whether "all" Gypsy wanted was to be a fad—the real actress was always lording it over her untalented sister in retaliation for accepting the handouts she got. "I want to be a legend. A fad is just one step along the way," Gypsy responded. But, she informed her sister, she had no illusions. The place where she was becoming a legend was not the Statue of Liberty or the Chrysler Building. Some New Yorkers, she said, made the pilgrimage there not only to see striptease or burlesque comedy, but to watch men masturbating under newspapers. "All the stuff they bring in with them—It's an education," said Older Sister to shock the woman formerly known as "Dainty Baby June."

But in addition to noting demographic details about her audience, Gypsy is also making a powerful social observation: striptease forced Americans to confront a greater degree of sexual voyeurism than many were ready to grapple with in public except as a "scare" or a perversion. Gypsy's understanding of the exhibitionists at the burlesque theater anticipates an icy decadence that is more at home in our era than it was in hers. Before she became famous, talking about stripping she sometimes sounds as though she has donned a suit of ill-fitting clothes. Or like Clark Kent complaining about having to be Superman. Yet the knowing quality in some of her confessions resonates more in our era than in hers.

The rise of café society buoyed Gypsy and pointed her social satire at the rich. Like the stripper's origins, those of café society are in dispute: the most popular version dates it to 1919, after World War I ended. Café society extolled public relations and nightlife over discretion and old money, going out over staying at home, fame over family, gossip over fact. By the crash, café society sent showbiz celebrities and old money, debutantes, wealthy men and women, movie stars, and musicians born on the Lower East Side to ferocious partying at Sherman Billingsley's Stork Club and El Morocco, as well as downtown at "the wrong places for the right people" like the eponymous Café Society. As Walter Winchell put it, "social position is now more a matter of press than prestige." In the Depression, photojournalism and gossip columns stoked the hunger for prestige and made bread-lines recede to the horizon the way the cowboy does at the end of the Western. While Americans starved and Okies wandered through the dustbowl, the *New York Times* reported a rumor that "fashion plate," ex-actress, and gay socialite Lady Mendl spent $40,000 a year on clothes. The new weekly pictorial, *Life* maga-zine, covered Brenda Frazier cavorting in New York and Coco Chanel wearing her couture in Paris. That in an era of extreme poverty a stripper should become the darling of café society—that she should become famous for joking about extreme ele-gance—not only illustrates our escapism; it also proves how op-posites attract in popular culture.

Nor were Gypsy's affectations in this era just mute admira-tion. The Queen of Burlesque adjusted her burlesque of the rich as though it were a corset that could be loosened, tightened, or unlaced. An important way to change the fit was the soundtrack. Whereas other strippers continued to disrobe to jazz and blues standards, by the end of 1934 Gypsy had added the "blue" lyrics of the gay Algonquin Round Table writer Dwight Fiske to her repertoire. This small adjustment, it turned out, would change her life. Born in 1892, Fiske (a.k.a. "King Leer") is worthy of his own book. He went to Harvard in 1912, then moved to Greenwich Village a few years later and began writing piano numbers for nightclubs. The Algonquin Round Table adopted him, and he became a hit at restaurants and clubs such as the Savoy Plaza, the Persian Room, and the Mayfair Yacht Club on Sutton Place. *Time* magazine described Fiske in 1933 as "lean, hatchet-faced, with hands like carefully manicured claws and a bald-spot on his narrow skull . . . hunched scornfully in front of a grand piano, intoning his unique compositions with an air at once chipper, elegant and insulting."

Time called Fiske's most famous numbers "sadly cruel little narratives of the aristocracy." There was "Mrs. Pettibone," a story of three failed marriages, and "Ida the Wayward Sturgeon," who, though a "modern woman," concluded: "There must be more to this sex-life than just swimming over each other's eggs." "Clarissa the Flea" told a story about an aristocratic flea who, after many travels, died when, as *Time* summed it up, "she tried to come between two HAPPY LOVERS."

Dragging Fiske's songs downtown recharged Gypsy's act. Carmel Snow, the legendary editor of *Harper's Bazaar,* asked Gypsy if she would pose for the magazine. Leonard Silliman cast her in his intimate revue, *New Faces.* After Gypsy performed in a benefit for the progressive City and Country School alongside celebrities such as George S. Kaufman, the *New York Times* called her "The Artist in burlesque."

"The Artist" became a fad. Critics deemed her speaking voice more compelling than that of Gladys Cooper, the British Shakespearean whom Aldous Huxley thought of as "stiff." She was "quicker on the uptake" than "naughty but nice" comedienne Beatrice Lillie, who specialized in Noël Coward revues and Cole Porter songs. But one review from the Irving Place era, in *Billboard*, mischaracterizes Gypsy by calling her the "Mae West of Park Avenue." Although the two stars both draw from the 1890s to deflect sexuality, they share little else. Whereas West used double entendres, Gypsy used the mot. Drawing on blackface minstrelsy, and drag, and encased in her hourglass dress, West painted seduction by numbers, while Gypsy, for all her acknowledgments of "thinking about sex," interested herself in acquisition rather than how-to. That same year, *Billboard* compared Gypsy to silent screen heroine Mary Pickford, acknowledging that nostalgia, as much as sex, drove the stripper's popularity.

By the fall of 1935, dressing the part helped secure Gypsy's role as a member of the cognoscenti. In November, at the opening night of Billy Rose's musical *Jumbo*, she wore a full-length ermine cloak, outdoing the New York and Hollywood stars who attended. In a publicity photo from that same era, she is wearing a hat of birds' wings that vanishes into her coif as if she were a hippogriff, which in a way she was. Or the stripper wears a lorgnette. O. O. McIntyre, in his column "New York Day-by-Day," reported that Gypsy is a "self-possessed lady with a cough drop voice and a dress suit accent who might have run up from Bryn Mawr for a prom."

Others scrambling up the social ladder may have been smart. But only Gypsy exploited American ambivalence about the intellect to satirize her carnality and her brain and her audience's expectations at every turn.

Gypsy's Imitators

Imitation is as much an idée fixe in American popular culture as is authenticity. But few other performers inspired so many different imitations so quickly in so many different mediums as Gypsy. In the 1934 Broadway season Fanny Brice and Imogene Coca had each portrayed goofy strippers with mysterious pasts. The following season, two bad plays about strippers opened there too. Yet artistic or box office merit is not the point. These qualities' absence proves that Gypsy's allure was linked less to artistry and more to an idea of how life was really lived in America. Robert Rossen, who would later direct *The Sting*, wrote *The Body Beautiful*, which *Time* praised for "contain[ing] some of the toughest talk heard on the Broadway stage this season, a trace of burlesque atmosphere, a strip queen . . . who takes pride in her work."

The idea that striptease could reveal more than just the body haunted writers. In several short stories published over the next year or so, Damon Runyon and John Cheever each used the figure of the striptease performer to demonstrate class injustice or other manifestations of hypocrisy.

In addition to the contributions of imitators and writers, the Queen of Striptease could not have been crowned without the effeminate gay men who were known at the time as "pansies." In the early 1930s, pansies had begun to congregate in burlesque theaters, where, as historian George Chauncey has documented, they met for liaisons. What Chauncey calls the "pansy craze" coincided with a vogue for female impersonation—gay men and women doing drag acts and singing and dancing and impersonating celebrities in 1930s New York. Gypsy knew that if one piece of her allure "pie"—the word she used to describe any financial deal—was slumming aristocrats, another was gay men who saw in her, as Broadway historian Ethan Mordden recently put it in an interview, "their poor, misfit selves" as well as a way to be "fabulous."

Gypsy solicited gay men's opinion and counted them as her friends. The admiration was mutual. A photo dated 1936 in the Gypsy Rose Lee Papers shows her mugging with female impersonators. Julian Eltinge, the Jazz Age female impersonator, asked for her autograph. Gypsy's use of Empire and Regency furniture, and her collision of highbrow and lowbrow elements in her act, owe a debt to her gay admirers. Other female stars were also influenced by (and themselves influenced) gay style. But whereas, say, Mae West burlesqued the female impersonator, Gypsy covered up, gesturing at revealing all, but then drawing back. (Both women elicited rumors that they were actually men in drag.)

Still, when gay men praise Gypsy, they sometimes sound as if they envy the ease with which she appeared to strip away social convention. Probably the nakedest airing of this emotion occurs in a *Vanity Fair* article written by Gypsy's gay friend George Davis early in 1936. Davis, whom she had first met in his Detroit bookstore ten years earlier, described the striptease star as "the dark young pet of burlesque" who "wins you at once, with her absurd Gibson girl coiffure, shirt waist, broad belt and flaring skirt, as she slips into the spotlight to twitter her sly way through Dwight Fiske's account of the marital misfortunes of Mrs. Pettibone." Davis moved from ridiculing Gypsy's costume and voice to exposing her as a not terribly bright poseur. "It is Gypsy Rose's fancy that the public of the Irving Place . . . revels in the double meanings of Park Avenue's favorite camp."

But Davis's take on his subject belies the glamour shot accompanying the essay. Hair in a French twist, Gypsy wears an off-the-shoulder Vionnet gown. Chin in hand, she tosses a sultry gaze at the camera, as if to say that she is only who you imagine her to be.

In the spring of 1936, a more enduring homage to Gypsy appeared in George Balanchine's ballet *Slaughter on Tenth Avenue*, a play within a play, and the sexy, violent act 2 finale to the Richard Rodgers/Lorenz Hart/George Abbott musical *On Your Toes*. Having arrived from Russia two years earlier, Balanchine was working in a showbiz idiom. Like other Russian émigrés, he had been fascinated with American popular culture from his student days in Paris. But *Slaughter on Tenth Avenue* is unique in its celebration and satire of a "Striptease Girl" (danced by Broadway star and ballerina Tamara Geva), a tap dancer (played by real-life tap dancer Ray Bolger), a murder, and the seedy club where she took it off.

"This was a takeoff of Gypsy Rose Lee, the stripper," Geva said in a 1978 interview with dance curator Nancy Reynolds. So when scholars of Broadway praise *On Your Toes* as the first musical where ballet and jazz function not just as virtuosic stunts or pretty sounds but as storytelling devices, they should also say that Balanchine made the striptease in *Slaughter on Tenth Avenue* into an archetypal American gesture. As critic James Harvey said of Ginger Rogers, who epitomized Balanchine's feminine ideal, "The Striptease girl is that mixture of displayed flesh and averted eye, both presenting and withholding itself at the same time." That mixture in *Slaughter on Tenth Avenue* makes it a coming-to-America story too. The Striptease Girl begins as a Russian émigré ballerina and ends doing a wild American striptease. But if you do a striptease, you cannot live happily ever after: The Striptease Girl's gangster-boyfriend, trying to shoot her lover, the hoofer, accidentally "slaughters" her. Everyone dies.

The real Gypsy preferred a twentieth century capitalist end-ing. That summer she judged a striptease contest at Leon and Eddie's nightclub on Fifty-second Street. Dressed as though she were going to a funeral—black veil, orchids diamond clip—Gypsy evaluated six contestants. *Variety* observed that striptease du jour was a "tormentedly yearning . . . type of dancing," with white-face makeup and a red gash of lipstick. To one critic these strip-pers parodied modern dance of a few years earlier, except that they bumped. *Variety* concluded: "GRL has raised the standard of striptease."

1936: A Stripteaser's Education

All celebrities have a vehicle in which they ride to embody their personality and the era and to fuse truth and fantasy in some new—or apparently new—way. For Al Jolson it was *The Jazz Singer*; for Ethel Merman it was "I Got Rhythm." Marilyn Mon-roe found *Some Like It Hot*. These vehicles elicit magic, a myste-rious melding of circumstances and personality. For Gypsy, her ditty "A Stripteaser's Education," in the 1950s sometimes called, after Freud, "The Psychology of a Stripteaser," or, at least once, "The Fine Art of Striptease," is this vehicle. Written by the lyricist Edwin Gilbert (and possibly Gypsy), "A Stripteaser's Ed-ucation" became so associated with Gypsy that sometimes the program just read "Gypsy Rose Lee Specialty." Everyone knew what she was going to do. Gypsy first sang "A Stripteaser's Education" after replacing Josephine Baker and Eve Arden in the Ziegfeld Follies of 1936. That she was said to be stepping in for both women reveals how big her range was supposed to be.

"A Stripteaser's Education" is many things: a stand-up act, a confession, Gypsy's most public revelation to date. Or should I say "revelation." That Gypsy put on a genteel approach to telling, using a sieve to allow bits of truth and falsehood to drip through the holes, elevated the mingling of a star's onstage and offstage life to a new complexity.

Thanks to the talkies, the 1930s were the first era in which stars could be "like us," and so Gypsy's tangling of intimacy and realism was not unique. But her offhand style, combined with stripping while confessing, made her exceed the revelations of many other 1930s stage and screen personalities, just as Paul Poiret's couture freed women's bodies more than corset designers ever imagined. Yet Gypsy's success would also entrap her, as all successes of this kind do. What liberates one generation enslaves the next. Gypsy talked about herself the same way she had circa 1936 after the charming gestures and static pose became stale. But that year despite her popularity, Gypsy was not an obvious choice to star on Broadway. But from one angle she was perfect for the role: she was a savior. The Ziegfeld Follies needed her as desperately as burlesque did six years earlier, for the Follies— the Jazz Age standard of revues—was on its way out.

The Shubert brothers (who had bought the Follies from Zieg-

Gypsy Rose Lee in the Follies. The Shubert Archive

feld's widow, Billie Burke) had gotten themselves into trouble. Failing to see that times had changed, the brothers conducted business as usual, stuffing the first edition of the Follies of 1936 with reliable old-school talent: Josephine Baker, the Nicholas brothers, Eve Arden, and Gypsy's old pal Fanny Brice. George Gershwin wrote the lyrics, Vernon Duke the music. George Balanchine did the ballets and Robert Alton the jazz dances. Yet only two hummable tunes emerged from the show: "Words Without Music," and "I Can't Get Started with You." The Follies ran one hundred performances and attracted mediocre reviews. Brice got sick; the show closed in May.

Another reason for the Follies of 1936's middling reception was that the Shubert's female lead, Josephine Baker, bombed. The Shuberts had overestimated New Yorkers' ability to accept sophistication in a female African-American performer. Critics judged Baker's costume as both too scant and too ornate. Whereas Baker had performed bare breasted in Paris, she wore pasties in New York, which might have reminded audiences of burlesque. Balanchine choreographed Baker in one number in a chorus of white men in Zouave uniforms. Another number, his *ballet d'action* "Five AM," cast the expatriate as an upper-class woman singing Gershwin's lyrics about longing, inspiring reviews bemoaning her ordinariness and decrying the possibility that a black woman could feel such delicate sentiments.

Although the Shuberts were desperate for a new female star, they were unsure that Gypsy could command a New York audience. *Variety* announced the Follies' reopening in September, with Gypsy listed as supporting Fanny Brice, and told of the Shuberts' intention to send the show on the road, where audiences demanded less. When the Follies opened at the Winter Garden Theatre, many critics were surprised at how good Gypsy was. *Variety* wrote, "Her striptease specialty is rather decorous but it rings the bell." Striding onstage in a picture hat with roses pinned to the crown, and wearing a floor-length skirt, "The flower of 42nd Street," as Gypsy called herself that year, sang-talked, spoofing sex, striptease, and her persona. Here are the lyrics to her signature number:

Have you the faintest idea of the private life of a strip-
Teaser? My dear, it's New York's second largest industry.
How a strip-teaser's education, requires years of
 concentration.
And for the sake of illustration, take a look at me.
I began at the age of three, learning ballet at the Royal
 Imperial
School in Moscow. And how I suffered and suffered for
 my Art.
Then of course, Sweet Briar, Ah those dear college days,
And after four years of Sociology,
Zoology, Biology, and Anthropology,

My education was complete.

And I was ready to make my professional Debut on 14th
  Street.

Now the things that go on, in a strip-teaser's mind

Would give you no end of surprise,

But if you are psychologically inclined,

There is more to see than meets the eye

For example—when I lower my gown a fraction,

And expose a patch of xxxx shoulder.

I am not interested in your reaction,

Or in the bareness of that shoulder.

I am thinking of some paintings,

By Van Gogh, or by Susanne [*sic*].

Or the charm I had in reading, Lady Windemere's Fan.

And when I lower the other side, and expose my other
  shoulder.

Do you think I take the slightest pride,

In the whiteness of my shoulder?

I am thinking of my country house,

And the jolly fun in shooting grouse,

And the frantic music changes, then off to my cue,

But I only think of all the things, I really ought to do.

Wire Leslie Howard, Cable Noel [*sic*] Coward

Go to Bergdoff's [*sic*] for my fitting, buy the yarn for
  mother's knitting

Put preserves up by the jar, and make arrangements for
    my church bazaar.
But there is the music and that's my cue,
There is really only one ting left for me to do, so do it.
And when I raise my skirts with slyness and dexterity,
I am mentally computing just how much I'll give to
    charity.
Though my thighs I have revealed, and just a bit of me
    remains concealed,
I am thinking of the life of Duce,
Or the third chapter of "the Last Puritan"
None of those men whose minds are obscene,
They leave me apathetic, I prefer the more Aesthetic,
Things like drams by Rossino . . . "Gone With The Wind."
And when I display my charms, in all their dazzling
    splendor,
And prove to you conclusively, I am of the female gender.
I am really thinking of Elsie de Wolff, and the bric-a-brac
    I saw.
And that lovely letter I received from Mr. Bernard Shaw.
I have a town house on the East River, because it's so
    fashionable
To look at Weflare [*sic*] Island, coal barges, and garbage
    scows.
I have a Chinchilla, a Newport Villa,

And then I take the last thing off,
And stand there shyly with nothing on at all.
Clutching an old velvet drop, and looking demurely at
  every man.
Do you believe for a moment, that I am thinking of sex?
Well I certainly AM

Most later versions of "A Stripteaser's Education" cleaned up the spelling and justified the margins. But in all versions, Gypsy teased Americans for believing her story about her origins and reminded them that she had become a success thanks to their suspension of disbelief. Most of the truths about her identity and origins were still too outrageous to be revealed while she was taking off her clothes, or at any other time. Even "A Stripteaser's Education"'s punch line, at which Gypsy claimed to be "thinking about sex," is itself a tease. Although at first it sounds like she replaces Victorian coyness with desire, sex is not the song's real subject; she always delivered this line with a wink. "A Stripteaser's Education" is less "Let's Do It" than it is "Song of Myself with Status Accessories."

Always aware of who she was stripping to, Gypsy used more erotic and opulent costumes and props than she had used downtown: garters and a long décolleté and backless velvet dress whose detachable mink sleeves could be turned into muffs as big as the Ritz. Yet although garters stood for sex, fur stood for wealth, and both would have amused and titillated a Depression-era Follies audience, neither of these props sent the same message that tossing pins and petticoats to working people did. You could say Gypsy depoliticized her act for the bourgeoisie or that using the muff and the garters—symbols from the world of the high-end brothel and the music hall—stripped her striptease of its most daring attributes. (This was the era of James Agee's *Let Us Now Praise Famous Men* and some of the most devastating poverty America has known.)

Still, in "A Stripteaser's Education" the Queen of Striptease did maintain one comic signature from the Irving Place—she kept the polka-dotted ribbons on her nipples. Overall, though, the number half-seriously asserted that the stripper was a universal ideal. As Chaplin transformed his tramp into Everyman, Gypsy turned the stripper into a democratic heroine. Like the Marx Brothers, Gypsy crashed high society's party, except whereas the upwardly mobile tuxedo-wearing jokesters who infiltrated the upper-class fete bounced to the curb, the Queen of Striptease was the guest who overstays her welcome.

Gypsy also performed a wide variety of comic supporting roles. In "Of Thee I Spend," a burlesque *Of Thee I Sing*, the 1931 Gershwin musical about presidential politics and sex, she played the incredulous Miss Gherkin. She sang "The Economic Situation"—a satire about the difficulty of getting a man during the Depression—and the Eve Arden part in her Gershwin duet with Bob Hope, "I Can't Get Started with You." Gypsy's take on "I

Can't Get Started with You" was typical. Whereas Arden had treated the Gershwin tune as a romantic number, Gypsy warbled her half of it for laughs. Bobby Clark sang the other half and the two ended in an acrobatic "burlesque kiss" which in Chicago became too acrobatic, and left Gypsy with a sprained ankle. Other roles included Fanny Brice's mother in "Baby Snooks Goes to Hollywood" and Dolores Del Morgan, a dame dancing "The Gazooka." Yet none of these roles ever became identified with Gypsy the way her striptease did. Throughout her career, whatever acts the Queen of Striptease tried, sooner or later in the evening the curtain closed and she came out front and took off her clothes, alone, sing-talking into a microphone. That was what audiences wanted to see.

Like all signature numbers, "A Stripteaser's Education" was a blessing and a curse. It condemned Gypsy to a career as an A-List B-List-er, a benchwarmer whom producers and directors could rely on to step into a celebrity role. Besides "A Stripteaser's Education" and its progeny, Gypsy performed mostly songs the great lyricists and composers had written for other stars. That she was always "singing someone else's song" lent her an air of comedy or tragedy, depending on the venue and the audience. Like Mae West, if she wanted her own tunes, she had to commission them or write them herself. Her failure to reveal herself made her words sound like impersonations.

Conceived as a gimmick, "A Stripteaser's Education" became

Gypsy Rose Lee and Bobby Clark. The Shubert Archive

a sexy joke, swelled into satire, and dissolved into camp where, because of age, much sexuality is forced to go. But the consistency of "Education" fails to console since it comes from a Peter Pan hope that neither she nor we will ever grow old.

When other performers took on "A Stripteaser's Education," the number became ordinary. Blonde chorus girl and Marx Brothers sidekick Marion Martin performed "A Stripteaser's Education" after she replaced Gypsy in the Follies in 1937, but no reviewers remarked on it.

As for Gypsy, no sooner did the Follies open than the press tore her down. "She undressed her way to fame," a headline read. Gypsy responded by distancing herself from striptease. She said it was dead. She rejected the honorific the "number one stripper." She said that her act "tickled peoples' funny bones" and that there was "nothing sensuous" about it. "I play my striptease for laughs," she told a reporter, as if by unsexing herself she could avoid rebuke. Here the impression is that she protests too much.

By this time Gypsy had developed a sixth sense for stroking the kingmakers. According to Erik, when she first arrived in New York she wrote Walter Winchell a thank-you note for mentioning her in his column after seeing her perform, but also confessed that he made her so nervous she would like him to see the act another night. Winchell obliged. Gypsy transformed her number into a three-dimensional version of his daily column. The publicity hound had met his match.

In 1936, when the Earl of Gosford, a guest of the Chicago "bluebloods" (as the press called wealthy Americans) the Otis Chatfield-Taylors, asked Gypsy out after a show, she made up an excuse about having to get up early the next morning to go to "an ethnological dance lesson." Gypsy added: "I was pleased with my performance." She regretted some of the things she had to learn to do for her new role, such as drink cocktails—she lacked the stomach for this—and smoke marijuana. But she never shirked her responsibility to her public.

Still, her success inspired swift and furious backlash. Even before the Follies opened, Alfred Eisenstadt, who photographed Gypsy for *Life* magazine on three occasions over the years, captured her leaning into the mirror, putting on her lipstick for a radio interview. Portraying Gypsy getting made up for a venue where no one could see her strip catches her dependence on artifice. But after the Follies opened, critics took umbrage to Gypsy's claim of being well read. It was one thing for a stripper to put on lipstick where no one could see her and make fun of café society, or to enjoy yachts and dining at chic restaurants. But it was too much to expect anyone to believe that she was reading the classics backstage. "It's said she discusses Joyce and Santayana at every opportunity—although I am at a loss to know just with whom she discussed these fellows with at Minsky's," one feature sniffed.

In an article in *Town and Country* titled "She Stoops to Conquer," Otis Chatfield-Taylor defends his friend as "the Gene

Tunney of Burlesque," after the Jazz Age boxer, friend of George Bernard Shaw, Yale lecturer on Shakespeare, and reader of *The Way of All Flesh*. He was not Gypsy's only supporter. Many newspapermen gave Gypsy the benefit of the doubt: she might not have read *Remembrances of Things Past* cover to cover, but she could talk about it at a party. Sometimes articles described her books as though they were stage props. She displayed copies of e. e. cummings and Joyce in her East Thirty-sixth Street duplex; the *New York Post* reported that she owned "5,000 volumes." *Life* magazine mentioned that Gypsy read Proust and Karl Marx in her dressing room, and another reporter noticed Dreiser's *The Genius*, Sherwood Anderson's *Dark Laughter*, and Vincent Sheehan's *Personal History* as occupying her bookshelves.

When Gypsy responded to the press's accusations, she brought up her working-class roots. "They think I'm some kind of freak," she told *Collier's* magazine shortly after the Follies of 1936 opened, referring to the American aristocrats who had made her famous and who were now turning on her. Gypsy's surface insouciance masks her understanding of a radical fact: the wealthy adore and resent being called out by the tough girl and guy personalities whose authentic American-ness they can only steal. The *New York World* reported that Minsky's, hoping its former star would come back, "installed earphones for the dowagers" supposedly flocking to the theater. Having succeeded on Broadway, the Queen of Striptease never wanted to go downtown again.

Slamming the People She Didn't Grow Up With

New York in the mid-1930s was full of rage against the American aristocracy, and nowhere more so than in the world of theater. The Group Theatre staged plays in which the working-class hero triumphed. Other groups invented new theatrical styles whose intention was to get the audience more involved; agitprop cast cartoon characters and stock settings to direct the audience's sympathy toward the ordinary man. Living newspapers used head-lines to draw attention to the economic and social injustices of the day. The stage was a pulpit on which actors preached social-ism. Clifford Odets's *Waiting for Lefty* premiered in 1935 and elicited a standing ovation for its depiction of working people suffering. But Gypsy's particular brand of beating up on wealthy Americans while flirting influenced the musical theater of this era as much as anyone in the serious theater. Take Harold Rome's 1937 revue, *Pins and Needles*, performed by and about the International Ladies Garment Workers Union. I find it difficult to look at Rome's title without thinking of Gypsy throwing her pins into the audience at the Irving Place. The revue included a skit making fun of a wealthy woman telling strikers, "It's not cricket to picket," and a Vassar co-ed "reduced" to working at Macy's.

In 1937 Rome was apparently taken enough with Gypsy to sell her one song, "For Charity, Sweet Charity," whose refrain includes the line "I Strip for Charity." I don't believe she ever sang it. But the following year Rome's revue *Sing Out the News* features a song about an anti–New Dealer "reduced" to eating domestic caviar that sounds like it is right out of Gypsy's playbook.

When Marc Blitzstein, who considered writing a show for Gypsy, describes what he was aiming for in this era, he noted: "I was slamming the smug people and traditions I grew up with." In an unpublished essay Gypsy described the socialite Anna Della Winslow advising her, "To satirize the rich you must know the rich." But because she was American, Gypsy never became La Pasionaria of showbiz. If she had been born in Berlin she would have become a serious theatrical presence like Lotte Lenya, who had arrived on our shores in 1935 along with Bertolt Brecht, already famous for *Threepenny Opera*. Known for talk-singing numbers, Lenya juggled high and low and sang of social corruption; Gypsy, with her fake past, mapped the difference between Europe and America. The Queen of Striptease reflects Americans' hunger for all kinds of revelations but particularly those linking flesh and commerce. The logical conclusion to striptease is constant: the performer ends up naked. So, like some captain of industry, Gypsy had to think about how to resell the same product every year while meeting consumer demand for novelty. In the 1930s she hired a shill to scream at the climax of her striptease to prove that, even if audiences called her a lady, she could play a tramp; in 1940, stripping for Mike Todd, having decided that the scream failed to convince, she added a waiter dropping a tray of dishes.

Gypsy was too interested in the anthropology of undressing to focus on something she considered irrelevant, like the color of someone's skin. She never achieved Paul Robeson's status, nor did she advocate for civil rights (unless you count those that her mother was always trying to take away from her). After 1936 she did perform at charity events in Harlem. And Gypsy also gave her maid, Eva, a part in her legend that was bigger than what most white celebrities of the time were willing to do. The story—that impresarios had offered Eva a role as a stripper but she turned it down—may be just another gimmick. But Eva functioned as Gypsy's dresser, played her confidante, and became involved in many aspects of her life—including the critical task of keeping Rose away.

In the months after the Follies opened, Gypsy scrambled between uptown and downtown, between her private and public roles. While she recited Noël Coward's "Don't Put Your Daughter on the Stage, Mrs. Worthington" for the Fleischman Yeast Hour, Rose was busy turning the Hovicks' past into sound bites. When June emerged, pregnant and broke, Rose, who had written off her younger daughter as dead when she eloped nine years earlier, engineered a tabloid story announcing "the confession of Gypsy Rose Lee's second sister." (In Rose's version June had not abandoned the family; the family had misplaced her in the hinterlands.)

The Queen of Striptease spent her nights polishing her paradoxical reputation. She attended columnist Heywood Broun's birthday party and frequented Sardi's, the Broadway celebrity restaurant on Forty-fourth Street, where she whispered salacious tales about her past in columnists' ears. She both consorted with and made fun of her old pal, Nudina, the Minsky's snake dancer, for wearing green gloves. When Billy Rose tried to lure her to his new nightclub, Casa Mañana, she declined. After hours, Gypsy gravitated downtown to "cafeteria society." She often finished evenings at the Howdy Club, a Greenwich Village drag club, or at Child's Restaurant on Fourteenth Street, a popular late night spot for gay men and theater people.

At the end of one of these nights Gypsy and Bob Mizzy, arriving home at 122 East Thirty-sixth Street, found robbers waiting for them in the foyer. The thieves absconded with $25,000 worth of jewelry, plus Gypsy's $16,000 mink coat. What is striking is not just that Gypsy was wearing that much jewelry (and so valuable a coat). It was that the press treated the theft less like a crime than like a new act the Queen of Striptease was trying out: "The bandits adroitly stripped Miss Lee of her jewelry," the *New York Times* wrote, as though the entertainer had made up the crime the way she made up her identity. Charles Bochert, a press agent, wrote to the paper to complain that the press's response to the theft revealed a shallow celebrity culture that had transformed a stripper into a socialite. "Had Miss Lee been robbed during her Minsky appearance, the incident would have been dismissed." That fall the *New York Times* and other papers mentioned Gypsy each time another society jewel theft occurred—and many did. Each mention dwelled on Gypsy's stolen jewelry, including a sixty-nine-carat sapphire ring and a fifteen-carat diamond and sapphire bracelet. Years later Gypsy would quip in her memoir that the jewel theft sold tickets to the Follies. But at the time the theft had a more immediate function: establishing the existence of Gypsy's diamonds and sapphires, it provided an overture to her next performance.

This time the stage was high society. Only a few days after the theft, Gypsy starred in the Beaux Arts Ball, an annual pageant for two thousand of the city's wealthy and privileged citizens, including Eleanor Roosevelt, the Vanderbilts, and the Morgans. Mrs. Stanwood Menken spent thousands of dollars on her costume and exhausted New York's supply of silver fringe. Held annually at the Hotel Astor, the charitable event donated proceeds to young architects. But as A. J. Liebling observed in a *New Yorker* "Talk of the Town" piece, what distinguished this ball from previous ones was publicity: it was funded by "an advertising man named Reimars, representing the American Enka Corp."

The ball hired many celebrities to entertain: John Gielgud and Gertrude Lawrence rode in on horseback. But the Queen of Striptease starred. For that year's theme—"the elements"—Gypsy wore a chiffon dress with a train representing "Eclipse of the Sun." Against a set of "the starry night sky," she took off the dress, which was festooned with paillard sequins as big as quarters, to Rimsky-Korsakov's "Valse Fantastique."

Would the reign of the Queen of Striptease never end? In December the *New York Times* warned readers about the "future Gypsy Rose Lees of this unembarrassed age." Just as the Statue of Liberty had become a symbol for freedom, Gypsy Rose Lee had become a symbol for striptease.

The Shuberts sent the symbol on tour with the Follies of 1936. When she arrived in Chicago this time, the Second City welcomed her. The *Chicago Daily Tribune* included Gypsy in its pictorial "What the Best Dressed Woman Is Wearing," captioning her "at work" to distinguish her from the other ladies of leisure depicted therein. But another picture from the same visit is captioned "The Duchess of Few Clothes." A review of her act observed that her striptease was "brief and cold blooded."

Gypsy was thirty-five, more or less. She did not match the "flapper" ideal of beauty, as arbiters of taste declared it in the 1920s, nor was she a curvaceous blonde like Mae West or Jean

Harlow. A word reporters often used to describe Gypsy was "statuesque," or, in the slang of the day, they referred to her "streamlined chassis." Or they wrote that she was "ethereal," which I think was supposed to be a synonym for smart. Her physical appearance was unlike any other actress on the scene. Her angular face never conformed to perky Broadway standards. Her sister writes that she disliked her long, elegant neck. But she glowered, darkly beautiful, flat-chested, and big hipped.

That year pictures of Gypsy project mischief. Maurice Seymour, the Russian émigré cum celebrity photographer, would take several cheesecake photos of the star that double as comic portraits. In one she hides her bare breasts with gloved hands while a black lace mantilla covers her head and shoulders, and she gazes away from the camera as though she were thinking wistful but important thoughts. In a newspaper photograph from the same era she wears a cutaway dress with red fringe covering her breasts, and she smiles like a grammar school teacher. What Gypsy wore in these photos deserves special mention because she became who she was in large part because of it. Since the Follies, her costumes leaned toward circusy spangles whereas her street clothes were haute couture. Entertaining reporters in 1937, she dressed in a pink and gray Rodier tea gown. Royer, who designed Shirley Temple's clothes, made for Gypsy a silver ball gown slit to the thigh.

THREE

To Hollywood and Back

Going to Hollywood raised Gypsy's status and alienated the Shuberts, who immediately placed an advertisement for a stripper—"no experience necessary"—in *Variety*. But many other Americans—especially New Yorkers—lampooned and celebrated Gypsy's ubiquity. Seniors at the prestigious Peddie School named her the "most prominent woman today," over Eleanor Roosevelt and Amelia Earhart. Comparing the stripper unfavorably to a well-known opera singer of the day, New York City Mayor Fiorello La Guardia bragged that the new airport being built in Queens "will be to Newark what Gypsy Rose Lee is to Kristen Flagstad." At a roast in City Hall, La Guardia, dressed as Gypsy, "tossed off the various clothes of the various political offices the mayor has been affiliated with."

Gypsy's success on Broadway attracted a more diverse group of impersonators. Female comics took it off, as they had in the mid-1930s, but now drag queens and African Americans joined them. Stumbling across the stage in Vincent Minnelli's 1936 revue *The Show Is On*, Beatrice Lillie hurled her garters, stockings, bra, and finally her wig into the audience from behind a chorus line. New versions of Gypsy emerged: an African-American Gypsy, a South American Gypsy, a drag Gypsy. As additional ersatz Gypsys popped up, popular opinion turned against the original. The *New Yorker* wondered if the *Daily News* was doing something treasonous by plastering the Sunday edition cover featuring her color photo on its trucks at the same time that La Guardia was outlawing burlesque in New York. The *Daily Worker* went even further, dismissing her as "a young lady who proves that the capitalist system is in the last stages of very beautiful decadence . . . she is what is quaintly known as a stripteaser, an art which has blossomed under the Depression whilst all else declined." Writer H. M. Alexander—who could be considered the Bill O'Reilly of his day—complained that after the Follies played in Kansas City, a department store's junior miss department sold a Gypsy Rose Lee zipper dress.

It was at the very moment that Gypsy supposedly destroyed striptease that writers began to see in it—and her—something quintessentially "American." The first pairing of the words "American" and striptease occurred that spring as something of a joke, when the Minskys testified before Congress that taking it off should be declared a national pastime, like baseball. "Stripping is definitely an American art," said Herbert Minsky, when he spoke before the House of Representatives House Immigration Committee. He and his brother Morton were called to testify at the request of Rep. Samuel Dickstein, the anti-Nazi activist from New York who had proposed two bills that would limit the number of foreign performers allowed to enter the United States. Many notable representatives from the arts and popular entertainment industry had already weighed in on both sides of the issue.

Herbert Minsky identified burlesque as "really the only school left for talent in the U.S." He concluded his testimony with a list of burlesque performers who had crossed over to Broadway and Hollywood, naming "last, but not least, Gypsy." According to him, the more Parisian chorus girls the government let perform their stripteases (as they were doing that very moment at the French Casino Theater in New York), the more difficult it would be for American stripteasers to achieve success. The press treated his testimony as a gimmick; opposed by both the Actors Equity Association and Sam Goldwyn, Dickstein's bills died in committee. But striptease and America were inexorably linked.

What about Hollywood? If Gypsy had stripped during her first sojourn there, her history—and that of striptease—might look entirely different. But in April of 1937 the woman whom Darryl Zanuck bought from the Shuberts for $20,000 arrived in Tinseltown to find that the Hays Office—the organization responsible for establishing censorship guidelines for the motion picture industry—was going to be as sympathetic to her as it had been to Mae West—that is, not sympathetic at all. A few years later, Gypsy recalled that Zanuck had sat her down and showed her "a stack of 20,000" letters from women who thought they were better qualified to act in the movies. (That the official number was 4,000 is one good index of Gypsy's relationship to the truth.)

But there is no exaggerating her failure. Gypsy arrived in Hollywood at a bad time for women. The longer the Depression dragged on, the more the Hays Office's so-called Production Code forced female stars to tone down the tough-girl personas they had developed in the earlier part of the decade. The problem began three years earlier, when the Hays Office passed the Production Code leadership to Joseph Breen, whose focus was on taming female stars. He enlisted a Catholic ally, the National Legion of Decency, and the hard times of the Depression to assist in his heavy-handed efforts. Mae West, who before 1934 had managed to evade the code by writing her own plays, found herself in its maw. The stripper who announced that her G-string was "diamond studded," a joke meant to allude to heiress Barbara Hutton's jewel of choice, was going to run up against the code—especially because this particular stripper had become famous by manufacturing her aristocratic pedigree.

"Hollywood Tames Gypsy Rose Lee," read a headline in the *Chicago Daily Tribune* at the beginning of May. Breen was not going to allow Gypsy to strip in the movies, just as he had ensured that Mae West would no longer sing her double entendres. Fearing that Zanuck was scheming to fashion his star into "a new Mae West," as well as hearing rumors that another striptease performer, Ada Leonard, would play Princess Zarina, a stripper, in the upcoming RKO production *Mrs. America*, Breen developed a sense of urgency in dealing with Gypsy. Twentieth Century Fox had forbidden Royer, its costume designer, to sew Gypsy anything risqué. A press release reported that the stripper had come down with "a case of the jitters" and that director Norman Taurog had to shut down the set. It appeared that Zanuck had lost this battle—or had he? When the studio declared Gypsy to be a "dramatic actress" and resurrected the name "Louise Hovick" ("Gypsy Rose Lee Finds Something Else to Shed," one headline read) to appease Breen, critics speculated that the Hays Office's strategy might backfire if Gypsy herself were to strip in a burlesque house while her first movie, *You Can't Have Everything*, was playing nearby. That would fill theaters. To compensate for not allowing Gypsy to strip on screen, the studio gave her twelve changes of costume, along with an elegant wardrobe for publicity stills. But even a brown suit of shadow-plaited cheviot, a tailored hat, and a full-length mink coat could not make up for the five bad films she would star in.

The Studio's maneuvering begs the question of why Zanuck hired what the National Legion of Decency called the "exemplar of what has most unfortunately become highly publicized under the degrading appellation of the striptease act" in the first place. Knowing Hays's power, Zanuck likely believed that, even incognito, Gypsy would equal box office success. As director Eddie Sutherland, who had tried to convince Paramount to snap her up a year earlier, told the *Los Angeles Times*, "Why if she only took her hat off in a movie it would be good selling propaganda."

But the Production Code censors wouldn't even let Gypsy take off her hat, so although Hollywood was making interesting movies in 1937–38, Gypsy starred in five duds. Of *You Can't Have Everything*, *Time* wrote that it was "bound to disappoint the admirers of Gypsy Rose Lee, whose sultry gifts are confined to such lines as 'I'll cut your heart out and stuff it like an olive.'" Filmed in the late spring of 1937, Gypsy's second movie, *Ali Baba Goes to Town*, startles by its campy badness: a hobo (Eddie Cantor) stumbles onto a movie lot producing an Arabian Nights fable. Cantor falls asleep and dreams himself into Baghdad, where, as sultan, he makes a new deal for his city before waking up. Gypsy plays the sultana. Perhaps casting Gypsy opposite Eddie Cantor, then a big star, was meant to soften a Hollywood fantasy about upward mobility's impossibility or to overturn the

satire she had been doing onstage for the previous ten years—
not to mention her real life story. Coiffed in a flat hairdo, Gypsy
does not so much act as spatula her dialogue into the scenes.

Gypsy's bombs sent a message from the Catholic Church to
American women: doing a striptease, no matter how ironic, not
only would prohibit you from playing the ingénue, it would en-
sure that you would wind up alone. In *You Can't Have Everything*
Gypsy, playing showgirl "Lulu Riley," the mistress of the roguish
George (Don Ameche), loses him to the chirpy, young, idealistic
playwright Alice Faye. The blonde next door will always van-
quish the brunette in furs. Not only does Lulu cheat on George,
she prevents him from becoming a real writer and tries to trick
him into marrying her. When one of the Ritz Brothers slaps
Gypsy's character across the face, he does so for a laugh. (Her
third movie, *Sally, Mary, and Irene*, was equally punishing.)

That the Gypsy who found stardom on Broadway in 1936
flopped in Hollywood a year later is no surprise. With few excep-
tions, female sirens typically did. Either they couldn't subsume
themselves into the characters that the studios wanted them to
play, or they attracted the morality police's attention, or both.
Hollywood declines to welcome women specializing in being
sexy and funny and destroys deviations from this rule—think of
Marilyn, the sexy-funny girl par excellence.

Gypsy defended herself by becoming a spokeswoman for a
modern attitude toward sex. She called Mae West "the weakest

link in the Vassar daisy chain." When Zanuck's lover, the actress Carol Landis, criticized stripping, Gypsy retorted, "I am sure no one will mind if she does Salome in long underwear and a fire helmet." And Gypsy's failure in Hollywood may have also made her more sympathetic to women. In America, then as now, mass appeal could come only with the fairer sex's Good Housekeeping Seal of Approval; women bestow that seal more easily on a woman who has lost as well as won.

The studio rewarded Gypsy for her cinematic failures. The *Los Angeles Times* listed her as one of the biggest money-makers in Hollywood that year. But in a column she wrote for Walter Winchell she complained, "I let them change my name . . . they gave me tragic eyes."

Only two months into Gypsy's tenure in Hollywood, scandal struck back East, and Rose was at the center of it. Before Gypsy left for California she had hired a young schoolteacher and art student named Genevieve "Jean" Augustin and moved her into Witchwood Manor, the lavish country house the stripper had bought for her mother. In June Augustin, whom Gypsy ostensibly hired to paint Rose's portrait and to serve as her driver, died of an apparent self-inflicted bullet wound during a party at the estate in June. The twenty-three-year-old from Kenosha, Wisconsin, returned from a hike, rigged up a revolver at the end of her bed, and, pulling the trigger with her toe, shot herself in the head. The story received much coverage. (Although Augustin's death was officially ruled a suicide, in 2003 Gypsy's son, Erik, told *Vanity Fair* that Rose killed her because she had flirted with Gypsy at a party.) As a result of the scandal, Rose came West.

Ten weeks later, having finished filming *Ali Baba*, Gypsy married husband number one, the handsome Bob Mizzy, who gets a bad rap in the various accounts of the Queen of Striptease's life. Not much is known about Mizzy except June's claim that Zanuck arranged the wedding to convince the Hays Office and the National Legion of Decency that his property (Gypsy) was no threat to American womanhood. June described Mizzy as "a lean, hungry wolf in the Disney tradition" and quoted her sister as calling her first husband "the most legitimate publicity I ever had." The press treated the wedding like what today we would call a starter marriage. Gypsy had to explain that she wed Mizzy on a boat to circumvent California law, which required couples to wait three days before getting a marriage license. But news stories covering the marriage reported that she was "too busy" to get married ashore, leaving the truth, whatever it was, to readers' imaginations.

My conclusion is that the wedding was more than a gimmick and that Gypsy's feelings for Mizzy were less venal than June claimed. Gypsy needed this man. When she overdrew her bank account, Mizzy transferred money into it. He was loyal, standing by her during all sorts of family dramas. He endured Rose's shenanigans even as he endured pressure from his own parents to stop fooling around with a stripper and take over the family dental supplies company.

Rose was worse. According to June, dressed in whiteface and rags she paid a visit to Zanuck to inform him that Gypsy was letting her starve. She also took to waving around a gun. But more consequential than Rose's dress-up act or her erratic behavior was the publication of a book holding her accountable for killing burlesque by promoting striptease. In this era, impresarios and writers reminisced about pre-striptease burlesque to announce their own virtue and decry contemporary venality, just as some Broadway aficionados wax nostalgic about musicals from the 1950s. The writer H. M. Alexander identified the villain. In *Strip Tease: The Vanished Art of Burlesque* (the most complete exposé of the burlesque industry), Alexander wrote that burlesque's golden age "was changed by a certain Mrs. Hovick. She was ambitious; she had a daughter; the child's stage name was Gypsy Rose Lee. When Mrs. Hovick still had to make Gypsy's costumes herself and cook all their meals on an electric plate, she somehow managed a rented limousine, a chauffeur, a bodyguard, and an ex-newspaperman who saw that it wasn't kept a secret from anybody. Publicity made Gypsy. When the stripper left Allan Gilbert's show at the Apollo to matriculate as a principal in the Follies, her former employers took startled notice, made a few inquiries, and hired press agents for themselves."

Thus, in one paragraph Alexander smites the mother and daughter team for destroying old-fashioned American values and for popularizing striptease—for turning something "sincere" into something "phony." A *Life* magazine photo taken on Gypsy's wedding day shows Rose, a brunette Medea in a housecoat, standing next to the newlyweds. Was this meek-looking woman with a pudgy chin and cruel mouth capable of destroying one theatrical genre and creating another? Wearing a beret and trench coat as though auditioning for a part in the gumshoe thriller that she would later write, Gypsy looks across her husband toward Rose and smiles. She appears to be listening to her mother.

After Gypsy's wedding, the family drove back to New York in her trailer. "At the request of Miss Augustin's mother" a grand jury investigation convened in Highland Mills. Nothing came of it, and Gypsy returned to Hollywood.

More bad films rolled out of Hollywood. Released in the spring of 1938, *Battle of Broadway* makes Gypsy the object of ridicule. Although she enters wearing a chic hat and a tight skirt, and an entire regiment shouts "wow," the joke is that the legionnaires mistake her character, chanteuse Linda Lee (two Lees!), for the girlfriend of the boss's son. Linda delivers the line "always a bridesmaid never a bride, but I love it." To make sure the audience gets that the old-maid singer is just a cinematic Gypsy, when the camera zooms in on Linda's photo album, there are photos of . . . Gypsy.

With Gypsy three thousand miles away, Rose deteriorated. The groundskeeper at Witchwood Manor complained about items disappearing. "I am not at all well the change of life is playing hard on me," Rose wrote to her daughter to justify taking the "oil stove from the living quarters, white wicker set from living quarters, garden hoe, rake, stove in basement, which was there to keep the tank from freezing, . . . electrical wire, . . . garage lawn chairs, lamps." The letters from Gypsy become icy while the ones from Rose seesaw between pleading and accusing.

"I was your slave and colored maid for years. I was never paid a salary," Rose wrote. "What did you tell June to make her hate me?" Gypsy replied in a telegram: "I have no desire to repeat last year's scenes. Your so called loneliness is of your own choice. . . . We just don't see eye to eye and that is final."

Hollywood failed to console Gypsy. Released that September, the Queen of Striptease's last movie, *My Lucky Star*, plotwise reprises her 1937 bomb *You Can't Have Everything*. As Marcelle Laverne, the woman who loses Cesar Romero to the ice skating champion Sonja Henie. She played the same shrew as she did in her first film. Just before Thanksgiving Gypsy decided to leave the West Coast for good. "After I'd taken a good long look at myself on the screen, I didn't like myself so well," she told a reporter. She further complained to a friend, the writer Douglas Gilbert, that all she had to show for her two-year sojourn was "a swell collection of autographs."

As usual, Gypsy's wit hides a piece of the story. She had also collected a good deal of material. But where to perform it? While she was making bad films in Hollywood, many burlesque theaters had closed due to anti-burlesque campaigns and the sour economy. Gypsy decided to launch a transcontinental tour, "the Merry Whirl Revue," in movie theaters and converted vaudeville houses. The tour began in San Bernardino and moved east. In Chicago, at the Palace Theatre for a week, she made $22,000 doing what *Variety* described as "a modified version" of her "Stripteaser's Education" number. The tour snaked through western and Midwestern towns destroyed by hard times.

But Gypsy did not do the tour just to remind Americans that she had become famous for her striptease. She had a more personal agenda: to redeem her time in Hollywood. As part of her routine, she sent an actor onstage to read a telegram: "she's been detained in Hollywood." She projected stills from her movies on a screen and then leapt through it as if to do via acrobatics what she had been unable to achieve via celluloid. Sharing the bill with Jimmy Durante, she played towns she had not seen since her childhood days in vaudeville.

Like Dorothy, who that same year enchanted American film-goers with her desire to go home in the *Wizard of Oz*, Gypsy wanted to tell Americans that she had only ever intended to use "Oz" to get back to Broadway. She introduced comic roles that inverted the usual Hollywood stories—such as the businesswoman "making advances at a timid male seeking a film test." Despite mediocre reviews, Gypsy's fans thronged to see her.

Small Town Farm Girl or Siren of the Burlesque Stage?
Back in New York in 1939, Gypsy needed more than the slip of a strap or a leap through a screen to reclaim her status as Queen of Striptease. Obsessed by the events in Europe, Americans had turned away from the arts in general and burlesque in particular. While Gypsy dallied in Hollywood, Mayor La Guardia closed all the burlesque theaters in New York and banned the word *striptease* from the marquees. The strippers who had plied their trade in burlesque in the mid-1930s had migrated to nightclubs. The acts had become more theatrical and more demure. Strippers performed gimmicks that would have been unheard of two years earlier, such as taking it off behind doves, balloons, snakes, or parakeets. But higher production values among strippers was not the only challenge that Gypsy faced: by this time, thanks to the talkies' growing popularity, the American theater had lost its place as the nation's primary form of entertainment.

Still, Gypsy put striptease to a good cause: helping the Spanish Loyalists, she joined artists and writers including Paul Robeson, Ernest Hemingway, and Robert Capa to raise money for the Abraham Lincoln Brigade, the mostly Communist American volunteer army fighting against Franco and Mussolini, and for Spanish refugees. At one benefit Gypsy told the crowd: "I have not come to lift my skirts, but to lift the embargo on Spain." When Gypsy headed a clothes drive at the Greenwich Village theater, the accompanying ad showed a photo of the half-naked stripper. The copy read: "Clothes? Any new clothes? Old clothes? Gypsy Rose Lee appeals for clothing for Spanish refugees . . . and she's not teasing. The artist who has given her ALL on stage and screen now asks you to give." Gypsy went on to describe barefoot, shirtless children.

What Gypsy saw as a gesture for a good cause, others regarded as a genius for the avant-garde. Barney Josephson told the *New Yorker* jazz critic Whitney Balliett that Gypsy had inspired Café Society, the soigné nightclub he would found the following year: "I'd seen Gypsy Rose Lee doing a political striptease at fundraising affairs in New York for the Lincoln Brigade. I conceived of the idea of presenting some sort of satire and alternating it with jazz music."

Intimates of the Striptease-Queen-turned-leftist-activist-muse were less impressed. Mizzy's mother scolded her daughter-in-law that she had "promised" to give up stripping, not to mention stripping for Communists. But La Gyp had no intention of giving up anything besides her marriage. She and Mizzy separated, and documents from 1938 (as well as press clippings) cite "extreme cruelty" as the reason.

Like many other left-leaning intellectuals and artists who helped the Abraham Lincoln Brigade, Gypsy attracted the attention of the Dies Committee, which had convened that year to ferret out Communists, especially those associated with the theater. But when the committee sought to question Gypsy, she wielded puns about her profession the way a lion tamer uses a chair. "I'll bare all if they come to Columbus," she told the press. The committee dropped its investigation, and at least one newspaper ran a story claiming that, by targeting Gypsy, committee co-chair Martin Dies revealed his own hunger for publicity. Perhaps he wanted to make it in Hollywood too.

Gypsy's reinvention during the war has sartorial and social roots. Thanks to the zipper's advent, getting out of one's clothes was more effortless than ever, as exemplified in the "Zip" number in *Pal Joey*, which opened during the 1940 Christmas season. A few years later Rita Hayworth teased in the film *Gilda:* "I'm not very good at zippers." That she never finished unzipping her evening gown provided a glimpse of Hollywood's double standard about the American striptease. No respectable actress could do one on screen—but every gorgeous woman was about to unsnap her garters.

The 1939–40 New York World's Fair exemplifies these changes. Held in Queens at what is now Flushing Meadows–Corona Park, the Fair promised "The World of Tomorrow," with exhibits of all kinds. As scholars have observed, the Fair offered several different visions of the American of "tomorrow." One was sanitized and technological. The other—the midway—was lascivious and vulgar. The midway included Norman Bel Geddes' "Crystal Lassies," topless women posing in G-strings, and the Cuban Village, where a completely nude girl did a voodoo act. Rosita Royce did her dove striptease. The press compared the area to Minsky burlesque.

In a "Reporter at Large" piece published in the *New Yorker* in the winter of 1939, Joseph Mitchell diagnosed a problem with the Fair's first season: Fair director Grover Whalen had not hired enough striptease performers. Particularly, Whalen had not hired Gypsy, which, he concluded, was "un-American." But Gypsy was not appearing at the Fair because she had received only one offer, and it was unacceptable. With the help of gallery owner Julian Levy, Salvador and Gala Dali had designed their own exhibit, "Dream of Venus," for the Fair's first season, and they invited Gypsy to star in it. At this moment the Dalis were in the middle of a love affair with American popular entertainment and especially with Hollywood celebrities. Salvador adored Groucho Marx, Buster Keaton, and Cecil B. DeMille films. Gypsy turned down the offer. No records remain of what she actually said, but perhaps the stripper intuited that although she and Dali may have shared a sense of publicity's function in twentieth century America, their ideas about how to do it differed.

The slogan the Dalis proposed to advertise Gypsy—"Come and See Gypsy Rose Lee's Bottom of the Sea"—drowned her in kitsch. And "Dream of Venus" would have cast Gypsy in a more outrageous role than any she had performed in, including the Irving Place. Fairgoers entered the Dalis' pastel-colored stucco pavilion, which was supposed to represent a dream, between a giant cast of a woman's spread legs. Inside, the Dalis had designed several rooms: in one, "mermaids" cavorted and drank champagne. In another, the Dalis installed a couch resembling Greta Garbo's lips, tossed in some Dali surrealist watches, and hired showgirls to play Botticelli's Venus. The Dalis imagined Gypsy as "the modern Venus," lounging in a boudoir filled with mirrors and mermen.

Having escaped the Dalis, Gypsy got cast in a crowd-pleaser— a Saratoga Circuit production of *Burlesque*, the 1927 Arthur Hopkins/George Manker Watters tear-jerker about Bonny King, a masochistic burlesque performer who makes it on Broadway and then becomes humbled and slinks back to her own genre. The Saratoga Circuit, an off-Broadway summer stock route, drew musical comedy actors like Vivian Vance and, now, Gypsy. Barbara Stanwyck had made the role famous in the original production, and by 1939 *Burlesque* had already been adapted to film twice. The stage revival, which hit Saratoga Springs the first week in August, during racing season, would have attracted many wealthy New Yorkers who traveled upstate to bet on the horses and take in the spa. *Burlesque* also gave Gypsy her first experience starring in a theatrical anti-rags-to-riches tale.

But in Saratoga Gypsy also got her first real taste of life among bohemians, as the town is home to the artist and writers' colony Yaddo. Founded in 1900, Yaddo was then run by Elisabeth Ames, who was known for her puritanism. Marc Blitzstein, whom Gypsy knew from New York, had holed up to work there, and he hosted a cocktail party in her honor. Fearing Ames's wrath, he held it at a studio known as the Tower, which was out in the woods, far from the main house. But perhaps Ames would have had nothing to disapprove of. According to the writer Jerre Mangione, who attended, Gypsy looked like "a wholesome small town farm girl" rather than "a siren of the burlesque stage." The party inspired Gypsy and drove her to seek out a similar life when she was trying to write her own book.

Wholesome small town farm girl? Siren of the burlesque stage? Who was Gypsy, really? At the very least, she was increasingly someone the cognoscenti wanted to tear down. In the fall of 1939 Gypsy became the third star of *Du Barry Was a Lady*, replacing the African-American mezzo-soprano Betty Allen, herself a replacement for Ethel Merman, who had joined *Panama Hattie*'s cast.

With lyrics by Cole Porter and a book by DeSylva and Herbert Fields, *Du Barry*, which had opened the previous December, was a popular hit (and a critical bomb) in part because it stole from burlesque. "One of the roughest books that ever headed uptown from Minsky," Brooks Atkinson wrote in the *New York Times*. Like *Burlesque*, the show Gypsy had starred in on the Saratoga Circuit a year earlier, *Du Barry* proposes the opposite moral of the stripper's real life story: America is not a place of social mobility. Cloakroom attendant Louis Blore (Bert Lahr) pursues May (Merman, then Gypsy), a nightclub singer, until he unwittingly drinks a drug-laced Mickey Finn and conks out. Dreaming that he is Louis XV, he finds himself in the same romantic situation: he chases May, now Madame Du Barry, around "Versailles." When Blore wakes up, he realizes that he and May should just be friends and that he should marry the cigarette girl who loves him.

The show demanded an actress who could approximate Merman's mix of wholesomeness and sex appeal in the contemporary scenes and also evoke the eighteenth century courtesan Madame La Comtesse Du Barry's naughty costume-drama hilarity. Although critics continued to dismiss *Du Barry* as a burlesque show in musical's clothes—Porter's "But in the Morning, No," was the kind of "sex" song Gypsy might have tried out downtown a few years earlier—Gypsy got good reviews: "lovely to look at and the comic sequences are good," one noted. Still, *Du Barry* was not the answer for an ex–populist stripper, ex–Hollywood starlet, ex–Follies star looking to reinvent herself. The Queen of Striptease needed a third act.

FOUR

The Rise and Fall of the Striptease Intellectual

An emblematic attempt to decrown the Queen of Striptease—to strip striptease of its elegant pose—occurred in the spring of 1940, when H. L. Mencken dragged Gypsy into a linguistic quarrel about her profession. This was classic Mencken: by calling attention to Gypsy's role in domesticating striptease, he would expose her and the "Booboisie"—his word for the aspirational middle class that had created her—as hypocrites. The spat began playfully enough when Gypsy's friend, the stripper Georgia Sothern, known for taking it off to the song "Hold That Tiger," set out to find a synonym for "striptease," as La Guardia had banned that word from New York burlesque marquees three years earlier. Sothern was Gypsy's striptease opposite. She neither pretended to be thinking about luxury products nor claimed to have attended Vassar. She got onstage and shook her body to loud music.

Sothern's campaign to play the amateur grammarian must have struck Mencken as even more ridiculous than Gypsy's intellectual striptease. Sothern sent letters to three intellectuals (Mencken would later claim her press agent, Maurice Zolotow, sent them): Stuart Chase and S. I. Hayakawa, popularizers of general semantics, a kind of analytic philosophy, and Mencken. The letter, in which Sothern cast herself as a stripper-in-distress, began: "I am a practitioner of the art of *strip-teasing* . . . there has been a great deal of . . . criticism leveled against my profession. Most of it . . . arises from the unfortunate word strip-teasing, which creates the wrong connotation. . . . [I]f you could coin a new and more palatable word to describe this art, I and my colleagues would have easier going. I hope . . . [you] can find time to help the . . . members of my profession."

Having first charted slang's direction in *The American Language* in 1921, Mencken had since been collecting words for inclusion in a second volume. Known by the 1940s as a lexicographer, Mencken aimed—as always—to eliminate pretension everywhere he found it. So he replied to Sothern's letter, which he would publish alongside his quips in his 1941 supplement to *The American Language* in high sarcasm. "I sympathize with you in your affliction. It might be a good idea to relate strip-teasing in some way to the . . . zoological phenomenon of molting . . .

which is *ecdysis*. This word produces . . . *ecdysiast*." Describing striptease as "molting" was like calling the middle class the Booboisie. What else could Gypsy do but rush to defend striptease's reputation? "Ecdysiast, he calls me! Why, the man is an intellectual slob! We don't wear feathers and molt them off. . . . What does he know about stripping?" she asked H. Allen Smith of the *World Telegram*. Mencken knew that Americans were turning away from striptease as Gypsy had defined it in 1936: as an amusing bauble and a critique of rags-to-riches tales.

Another incident from that same spring reveals a Gypsy out of touch with her public. In her memoir, *Talking Through My Hats*, the milliner-to-the-stars Lily Daché tells how, in May, one month after Mencken and Gypsy tangled, the stripper was the guest of honor at a benefit for the United Committee for French Relief. Held in New York's chic Ritz Carlton Hotel, the event promised to be "one of the great fashionable occasions of the season." Frank Crowninshield, the editor of *Vanity Fair*, emceed. Society matrons, debutantes, and celebrities from all milieus attended. Gypsy wore a striped silk dress with removable panels, but it does not seem that the entertainment committee had planned for her to strip. The evening was proceeding calmly until, as Daché told it, "someone whistled." From then on, no one could stop Gypsy from taking off her clothes. Even Mary Pickford, who at one point offered her $700 if she would keep her skirt on, failed to dissuade her. But in the middle of her impromptu striptease, Gypsy suddenly stopped stripping and strode backstage. Daché, who followed her, recalled: "there she was, in a mink coat, a hat on her had and one in each hand. 'Look I'm ready,' she said. 'Ready for what?' I asked. She threw open her coat and there she stood in her famous G string and bejeweled brassiere. On each side of the brassiere she had pinned a hat, and another in the middle of the G string." It was at that moment, Daché adds, as though to contrast the narcissistic stripper and the world-shattering political events in Europe, that the radio broadcast the news that Germany invaded Holland.

Gypsy next signed with the young entrepreneur Mike Todd, who was looking for a star to replace Carmen Miranda, the "Brazilian Bombshell," in *Streets of Paris*, the hit revue that the Shuberts had produced at the Broadhurst Theatre the previous year. It was a tough act to follow. At that time Miranda, with her flamboyant fruit headdresses and aggressive cha-chas, commanded the highest salary of any female star in America. To make audiences forget her, Todd plastered Gypsy's image on a forty-foot-high billboard and boasted that she was "bigger than Stalin" (that remark had not yet become an atrocity). He charged audiences $1 to see her, more than the price of admission for any other show.

Gypsy succeeded at the Fair not just because of her forty-foot billing, Todd's absurd publicity claims about her, or the exorbitant price of admission. She succeeded because she was able to transform her high/low persona from the 1936 Follies into a patriotic-comedic one to tell a fresh, yet familiar, story. At the time, Germany was occupying France, and Gypsy proposed an evening of diversion by reprising some of her old burlesque routines and introducing new ones to update her fans about her own story. She did an abbreviated version of her signature striptease, which *Time* magazine described as "absent-minded." She was by now a master at turning rumors into revelations about herself, especially those that poked fun at her legend.

Whereas in real life Gypsy played a stripper sprinkling her routine with French phrases, in *Streets of Paris* she played an American pretending to be French in "The French Have a Word for It." That she mangled the language cast doubt on her "elite" image, or at the very least presented it while winking—"*Voos ette aytrainjeer a Paree?*" (Are you familiar with Paris?), she asks the other equally clueless dame. In another number, as "the widow" in one of burlesque's most famous skits, "Floogle Street," playing opposite the young comic geniuses Bud Abbott and Joey Faye, Gypsy torments the delivery boy with a bump before smashing one of the hats he is trying to find a home for. (The gag is that everyone the boy meets goes nuts when he says "Floogle Street" and destroys a hat, so that at the end of the skit he has no hats to deliver.) And in "Robert the Roue from Redding, Pa," which Bobby Clark had sung in *Streets of Paris* the previous year on Broadway, Gypsy satirized a rube who came to the city to become a "wolf."

For *Streets of Paris* Gypsy attracted a less elite audience than the one that had carried her to fame in 1936. Upper-class New Yorkers came to see Gypsy but so did the character that *Time* called "Elmer," meaning the average American citizen, although it is unlikely that Elmer recognized the black gown with a padded fishtail as a Schiaparelli that Diana Vreeland had loaned her. The haute couture mermaid/populist stripper inspired *New York Times* theater critic Brooks Atkinson to call her "tall, sleek and mischievous" before he withdrew to pronouncements about the dangers of making light of sex: "Humor in strip-teasing is in questionable taste. Some things are too sacred to be kidded." The *New Yorker* disagreed. Kidding sacred things was the point. "We want to watch . . . Gypsy Rose Lee return as nearly as possible to the condition of her birth. At the end of a strip tease we demand spiritual comfort, not H. V. Kaltenborn," the magazine opined, referring to the radio commentator who had become "the voice of the war."

Streets of Paris also gave Gypsy her first opportunity to put her dreams of reinventing herself as a literary figure into practice. In August she guest-wrote Walter Winchell's column while he was on vacation, satirizing the sentimental ideas about men and romance circa 1940. She divided the column into sections: "The Men I Love" (those who had given her starring roles); "Orchids and Notes" (presents); "First Breaks on Broadway" (career). She would later cite the column as giving her the confidence to write her first book.

Gypsy also met the next "man she loved"—the short, swaggering impresario Mike Todd—at the Fair. Until 1990, when Erik Preminger donated his mother's papers to the New York Public Library for the Performing Arts, Todd's children and biographer Art Cohn denied the affair. Since the Gypsy Rose Lee Papers contain Todd's love notes, their relationship is irrefutable. I have often wondered if the denials are so vehement because Gypsy was a stripper.

Todd was no choirboy. He was one of those larger-than-life figures in the American theater who have vanished with the egg cream. Born in Minneapolis around 1907, Todd sold newspapers, shined shoes, played a cornet in a boys' band, ran a general store, and became an excellent craps player before he was twelve. When the Todds moved to Chicago, Mike worked as a carnival pitchman, shoe salesman, soda jerk, pharmacist, and president of the "Bricklaying College of America." He ran a road show whose star was a trained penguin and wrote gags for a vaudeville team. At the 1933 Chicago World's Fair Todd produced a striptease act "the Moth and the Flame," in which a ballerina in a tiny costume (moth) threw herself at a flame. He also was a salesman who leased "Kute Kris Kringle"—a miniature Santa Claus—to department stores. His idea was that children could peer inside a dollhouse window, see Santa inside, and speak to him on the phone. But Todd was not just a hack. He was also interested in Ferenc Molnar, the Hungarian writer whose play *Liliom* later became the musical *Carousel*.

In the first season of the 1939 World's Fair Todd produced an updated version of *The Mikado*, with Bill ("Bojangles") Robinson. During this time (Todd was still married to his first wife, who would shortly die under mysterious circumstances) along came Gypsy. It is often said that Gypsy saw in Todd a male version of herself, as though her story reset that of Narcissus and Echo on the Great White Way. One story tells how Todd fell in love when he caught Gypsy cooking knockwurst in her dressing room to save money. But while the two carnivorous skinflints were both larger-than-life showbiz people who scrambled up from nothing and triumphed in the golden age of Broadway, their attraction revolves around more than a taste for Jewish deli food and for gazing at each others' reflections. Todd's savvy and machismo won Gypsy. She fell so hard in love with him that, for her, she did the unthinkable—in addition to marrying someone else to make him jealous, that is—she lent him money. She would agree to be an angel for the 1942 musical *Star and Garter,* which they co-produced and in which she starred. As usual, June explained her sister's attraction in mercantile terms: "Mike picked up the myth machine where Eddy had left it" and quoted Todd's marveling that "a stripper who don't strip" could attract so much attention as though it proved his disregard for her sister. Such cynicism overlooks Gypsy's passion for the man who bore more than a passing resemblance to Edward G. Robinson. Why didn't they marry? Since the two were married to showbiz, perhaps neither one was interested in breaking up. Or perhaps, as Erik once wrote, his mother knew that Todd had a mean streak. Nonetheless, the affair continued for almost four years, and letters and telegrams in the Gypsy Rose Lee Papers confirm Todd's sweetness and passion.

The G-String Murders

Just before he set off across America in the fall of 1940, Henry Miller wrote, "Gypsy Rose Lee (burlesque queen) saying to me at World's Fair, N.Y. on eve of trip: 'I could think of a lot better things to do than tour America.'"

She found that thing in the world of letters. After the Fair ended in the summer of 1940, Gypsy left her apartment on East Fifty-seventh Street, her antiques, and her Chinese maid for the third floor of a house on Seven Middagh Street in Brooklyn Heights. Many writers, including Sherill Tippins, the house's biographer, have since described it as an artist's colony—even Yaddo South (it was torn down in 1945 to make room for Robert Moses's Brooklyn Queens Expressway). But although Yaddo shares with Seven Middagh the berthing of a wide range of literary and artistic luminaries—David Diamond, W. H. Auden, and Benjamin Britten all spent time at Seven Middagh—and a reputation for sexual shenanigans, to my knowledge Yaddo has never welcomed a neighborhood character nicknamed "Ginger Ale," who played ragtime piano nude, a lit cigarette in his butt. Also,

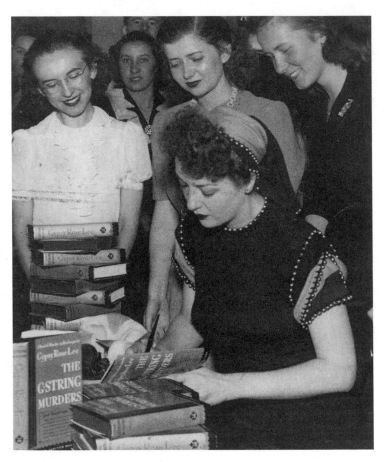

Gypsy Rose Lee autographing copies of her novel *The G-String Murders*, ca.
1941. Billy Rose Theatre Division, The New York Public Library for the
Performing Arts, Astor, Lenox and Tilden Foundations

compared to Yaddo's totalitarian administration at the time, the management at Seven Middagh was positively louche.

Lincoln Kirstein wrote a small check to pay rent. But the muse behind the impresario was George Davis, Gypsy's friend, a magazine editor who embraced with such fervor the idea of bringing serious writers to popular magazines in the 1930s that he was fired from every editorial post he held—well, that and his disheveled comportment in the offices of *Harper's Bazaar* and elsewhere. *New Yorker* correspondent Janet Flanner described him as "a sulky, extra sensitive character and a deadly wit." Other denizens of Seven Middagh included, not all at once, Carson McCullers, Richard Wright, Paul and Jane Bowles (recovering from Morocco), as well as Thomas Mann's son Golo. Salvador and Gala Dali, George Balanchine, and Kurt Weill dropped by, as did Flanner, who would introduce Gypsy to her publisher, Simon and Schuster. The portrait photographer Louise Dahl Wolfe, another photographer who did her part in immortalizing Gypsy in domestic settings, met the stripper there. Thomas Mann's other children, Klaus and Erika, spent a festive Thanksgiving dinner at the house and may have at least partly inspired Gypsy to donate some of her papers to Princeton University's Firestone Library.

Reactions to Seven Middagh oscillated around Gypsy or George, who told the poet Harold Norse how he liked the Brooklyn port and the Bucket of Blood bar on nearby Sands Street, where he chatted up sailors and then seduced them. Caroline Seebohm wrote that Seven Middagh was "odd but it was lively." Peter Pears called it "sordid beyond belief," and Louis Untermeyer noted that Seven Middagh was "gay (in both senses of the word)" and that "Gypsy did not strip, but Auden did plenty of teasing."

Seven Middagh may have both stifled and inspired Gypsy. In 1941, back on the road and working hard, she complained about late nights giving her "the Yaddo pallor." More of a home than Gypsy had ever cozied up to thus far, Seven Middagh was no Party Central or not just Party Central. Gypsy got work done and became a muse to Carson McCullers, who had already published *The Heart Is a Lonely Hunter* to much acclaim by the time she arrived there. McCullers finished *The Bride and Her Brother*, the working title for *The Member of the Wedding*, after a fire woke everyone in the middle of Thanksgiving night. Running down the street holding Gypsy's hand to see the fire truck and the burning building, McCullers realized what was missing from the novella. She shouted: "Frankie is in love with her brother and his bride and wants to become a member of the wedding." According to Carlos Dews, a McCullers scholar, the relationship between the two women went further than hand-holding housemates. But I think it is more likely that the fragile writer imagined the affair.

Seven Middagh's heady intellectual atmosphere would not have been new to our heroine. Since Gypsy first arrived in New York she had cultivated a diverse group of friends and acquaintances, including gangsters, their molls, Broadway producers, illustrators, columnists, and designers. That she still continued to consort with gangsters reveals the attraction that the underworld held. According to McCullers, Waxey Gordon, the thug-turned-bootlegger who had gotten Gypsy her first Broadway role, showed up at Seven Middagh upon his release from Leavenworth in 1940. He stationed his bodyguards in the street next to his black Packard, spent the night, and stashed money for Gypsy under the doormat.

But until Seven Middagh the majority of Gypsy's intimates came from theatrical circles: Ward Morehouse, the theater critic George Jean Nathan, the illustrator Marcel Vertes, whose sketch of Gypsy at her typewriter on her stationery defined her. At Seven Middagh Auden presided over the meals, but Gypsy served joie de vivre and gave domestic advice. She installed her cook, Eva, a former Cotton Club chorine, in the kitchen, to cook roast beef. A six-foot cardboard cutout of Gypsy from the Irving Place Theatre decorated the living room. Gypsy "came around for meals like a whirlwind of laughter and sex," wrote Louis MacNeice, a frequent guest at the many raucous dinner parties at the house. Gypsy excelled at parlor games like Charades and the Yaddo favorite, Murder. During a Thanksgiving party she perched on the lap of Benjamin Britten's patron and friend Michael Mayer, holding a bottle of gin.

Besides being a good sport, Gypsy contributed financially to Seven Middagh's upkeep. In contrast to the writers and composers there, she was a wealthy woman. But she nonetheless spent her days at Seven Middagh hard at work on her first thriller, *The G-String Murders*. The house inspired the stripper to get the story of her life down on paper in a way that—though still fiction—was more truthful than any skin she had flashed on stage.

Gypsy would spend the next two decades retelling this story: first as a detective novel; then as autobiographical tales in the pages of the *New Yorker, Harper's Bazaar*, the *American Mercury*, and elsewhere; and finally, much later, as her full-length memoir, *Gypsy*. From the first she approached her new craft the same way that she had approached her old one: as a comic striptease where she withheld most of what she knew while dangling a few choice limbs in front of her audience. She called writing "mak[ing] with the book words."

Writing exhausted Gypsy. Plus, Mike Todd continued to woo her. He wrote, "I left too early to wake you, darling." And, "your mind is more beautiful than your body. Or vice versa," he wrote from Chicago, shortly after Thanksgiving. And, "I'm lonesome."

Around the holidays Gypsy gave in. She headed for Chicago to star at Todd's Theatre Café, a profitable venue that Todd had opened in a jai alai palace in a decrepit part of town. Until June, when the authorities decided that gangster Frank Nitti had bankrolled it, the red, white, and blue café, located at the corner of Clark and Lawrence Streets, featured vaudeville shows, sat 3,700, and employed 190 waitresses, 100 entertainers, 2 dance bands, and 25 bartenders who manned a 400-foot-long balcony bar. Todd served dinners for 75 cents and a champagne cocktail for a quarter, although he banned dice games and "B-girl" hostesses. Gypsy described stripping there as a family event: "I'd be out there doing the number and the kids were swinging back and forth on the railing."

While Gypsy was pleasing the family crowd, the culture was hardening against striptease. Richard Rodgers and Lorenz Hart's *Pal Joey*, which opened at the Ethel Barrymore Theatre in New York, illustrated how sympathy shifted from Gypsy. Written by John O'Hara, the work, originally published as a short story in the *New Yorker*, became the musical that kept Gypsy in the public eye. But it also showed how Americans were coming to see striptease as a gimmick. The casting was also a Hovick family affair. June played Gladys Bumps, the corrupt chorus girl. According to June, Rose called on the producer, George Abbott, accompanied by, as the younger daughter wrote, "a les." Rose wept and complained of hunger, deprivation, and daughterly abandonment.

Besides offering a stage for the Hovick women to play out the roles they had constructed offstage, *Pal Joey* presented the striptease intellectual as a hoax. Rodgers and Hart give Gypsy's number to the journalist Melba Snyder, to sing in the number "Zip," just after Joey, the sleazy emcee, has told his own series of whoppers about his wealthy past. Melba doesn't take off anything. (No one does in the musical.) Instead, she responds to Joey's chicanery with a tale about the "funniest" person she has interviewed—Gypsy Rose Lee, whose striptease is a gimmick. The point of the pissing contest: Striptease is a less vile con than the others occurring onstage right in front of her.

Zip! Walter Lippman wasn't brilliant today.

Zip! Will Saroyan ever write a great play?

Zip! I was reading Schopenhauer last night.

Zip! And I think that Schopenhauer was right.

I don't want to see Zorina,

I don't want to meet Cobina.

Zip! I'm an intellectual.

I don't like a deep contralto,

Or a man whose voice is alto.

Zip! I'm a heterosexual.

Zip! It took intellect to master my art.

Zip! Who the hell is Margie Hart?

"Can you draw sweet water from a foul well?" Brooks Atkinson famously asked about *Pal Joey*. You could ask the same question about Gypsy. When *American Mercury*, the magazine founded by H. L. Mencken and George Jean Nathan, named Gypsy "The Striptease Intellectual" in a feature article, this new moniker evoked a version of that question: was the phrase an oxymoron or did it expose a rags-to-riches truth?

Gypsy either ignored these debates or exploited them. To show support for the troops she wore a net bodysuit spangled with stars, or a Merry Widow with stars sewn in the bra. In this costume on New Year's Day of 1941 at a benefit for the British War Relief at the Astor Hotel in New York, Gypsy made the cover of *Life*. A photo inside the magazine showed the industrialist William Rhine-lander Stewart plucking a star from her bodysuit, as the caption described it, "for $10." But the following week the mayor of Youngstown, Ohio, wrote in to inform the editors that he was banning that issue from his city.

Americans appreciated Gypsy most in this era, when, reprising her prewar act, she contrasted her fake elegance and her vulgar surroundings. Comparing her to the torch singer Marion Colby, Cecil Smith, who would later become the *New Republic*'s music critic, praised her refusal to invest striptease with what he called "phony emotionalism." He meant that she did not pretend that she liked to strip. Maybe Gypsy took his advice to heart. On the road, finishing *The G-String Murders*, Gypsy invested letters to her editor Lee Wright and her publicist Charlotte Seitlin with an irreverent quality. In these letters, which Simon and Schuster would later send to reviewers, she does what she did best: casting herself as an ingénue in a sordid setting for comic effect. But she also used gender: in one letter to Wright in 1941, she both flirted and complained as she discussed her detective story in which burlesque people used showbiz jargon, yet her editors wanted her characters to talk like Park Avenue doyennes. Would they have asked that of Damon Runyon? she wondered. She signed off, "The Naked Genius," or "The Girl with the Diamond Studded Navel." She poked fun of the particular ironies of her double-casting. From Chicago she joked that "you see it takes almost an hour to soak off my body paint so I do my rewriting while I wait" and that using a blue ribbon on her typewriter enhanced her sex appeal. But Gypsy also stood up for herself, objecting when Wright tried to turn the murderer in *The G-String Murders* into a madman. "That annoys *me* too much when I'm reading a mystery."

While the press coverage of Gypsy often blamed literature for her intimate life's failures, those close to her relied on amateur psychology to explain the same. After her divorce from Bob Mizzy was finalized in March, Gypsy was quoted as saying that the couple parted ways because of a difference in temperament: whereas Mizzy wanted to go nightclubbing, she wanted to sit home and read Somerset Maugham. That made her sound silly or insincere. But in a letter June's then husband, Jesse, ventured her theory about the separation. "Bob's inferiority complex was pretty heavy. . . . And when one of the two [married people] is an actress, the other must accept that fact and be generous with his patience, and occasionally forget that arrogance and noise are not necessarily virile." It's more likely that Gypsy was a work in progress.

That summer, when Gypsy asked the International Longshoreman's and Warehousemen's Union for $500 for the war effort, Harry Bridges, the union's controversial Communist leader, said he had to investigate the USO campaign before parting with the money. Gypsy stood up, shook her fist, and shouted: "Our men need the money now." Bridges called her a "political menace." The anti-Communist press reported on her action as a kind of patriotism. Otherwise most of Gypsy's efforts for the war had gone smoothly. She performed at benefit events for starving children and at a rally to support striking cosmetic plant workers. She uncomplainingly sold war bonds and did USO tours to boost soldiers' morale. In 1940 Gypsy had judged a beauty contest in Harlem and performed at the Apollo Theatre alongside stars including Billie Holiday and Ethel Waters, and she also gave money to the Red Cross. But Gypsy's fit of pique at the Longshoremen's Union reveals a woman in search of a new role. She had not yet become a writer. But she was no longer a stripper, even an aristocratic one.

Just before *G-String* was published, photojournalist Eliot Elisofon documented Gypsy's transformation from the Queen of Striptease to the Striptease Intellectual for *Life* magazine. Elisofon, who, according to gossip columnists was dating Gypsy, shoots the celebrity in what, for her, would have been an unconventional setting. She is neither backstage nor taking off her clothes onstage. She is turning the boring and unphotogenic act that intellectuals all over the world do—writing—into performance art avant la lettre. Sheets of paper cover the Aubusson rug. Gypsy wears pants rolled up to her knees, and she is barefoot. Her hair is pulled back into a messy bun. She is holding a cigarette, and ashes overflow from the ashtray onto her desk.

Although Gypsy mastered this photo opportunity with the same sure hand that she had mastered previous ones, I do not think that she ever imagined that *The G-String Murders* would be such a wild commercial success. But Gypsy may have intuited what kind of book that she could turn into a hit. Rather than aspire to serious literary fiction, she had the good sense to write a thriller at a moment when Americans considered that genre less literature than burlesque for readers. Published in October 1941, *The G-String Murders* is a memoir posing as a thriller, revealing Gypsy's life in peekaboo glimpses. The heroine, "Gypsy," refers to herself, among other things, as "the dazzling star," a phrase that she stole from a tabloid account of her arrest in 1931. Gypsy disguises the theater and many of the other characters' names, but only barely. There is a greedy burlesque owner, a lesbian policewoman, and Princess Nirvana, a stripper with intellectual pretensions.

Critics complained that the book's content was risqué, and for the time it was: Gypsy describes how the strippers keep their breasts from sagging (splash ice water on them, resort to dangerous paraffin implants). The murderer strangles several victims with a G-string. But more interesting than the naughty bits is that Gypsy tells the story in the first person, as though rehearsing for the memoir she would later write.

Although *The G-String Murders* immediately hit the bestseller list, was reviewed more than five hundred times, and eventually sold about twenty-six thousand copies, more than any other thriller at the time except *The Thin Man*, Simon and Schuster initially promoted it as "well constructed." This shows about the same degree of confidence in Gypsy as Stephen Sondheim did when he described Ethel Merman as a "talking dog." But in one of her many deft moves of that era, Gypsy herself quipped, in a review of her own book for the "Down the Aisle" column, that she didn't know why critics were making such a fuss. *The G-String Murders*, she wrote, flashing her literary knowledge even as she covered it up, "isn't even *Crime and Punishment.*"

Whereas Gypsy's success on Broadway had inspired the press to doubt her claims about reading, her success in publishing made them doubt her past itself. Reviewing the book for the *New*

Yorker, Clifton Fadiman characterized it as better read "with eyebrows raised." *Daily News* theater critic Burns Mantle wrote that since the book was "readable," Simon and Schuster "wrote *G-String* and Gypsy checked it." (He retracted this statement after Gypsy wrote him an angry letter.) Never a fan, the *Daily Worker* called the book "a stunt."

But in March 1942 Gypsy, along with many other celebrities, performed for the opening ceremony of the Victory Book Campaign, which donated copies of books (including Gypsy's) to the troops. It is testament to how thoroughly Gypsy had become mainstream that, reversing his criticism of the star at the 1939 World's Fair, Brooks Atkinson commended her for making striptease "as American as hot dogs . . . Gypsy had as much right to speak from the steps of the library during the Victory Book Drive as many other authors less famous for their pleasing style," he wrote.

Still, no matter how Gypsy sparkled in public, she could never overcome the suspicion that she was faking her literary talent. That may have been part of the appeal. Assaulting received wisdom about the stability of class and gender, the phrase "Striptease Intellectual" inspired snickers and glee. "Gypsy Rose Lee has not only written books, but read them," the *New York Herald Tribune* opined in 1942. But Gypsy did read books, although her taste sometimes wavered according to her social compass. She liked Tennessee Williams's play *Camino Real*, as well as *Waiting for Godot, Desire Under the Elms,* and the sentimental novel *I Can Get It for You Wholesale,* by her friend Jerome Weidman. This last choice is interesting. In Weidman's novel, a Depression-era immigrant makes it out of the ghetto. Harry Bogen succeeded by his wits—the "act" that Weidman writes about is a kind of male, Jewish Stripteaser's Education. Maybe every American novel is.

The charge that *The G-String Murders* was ghostwritten, which has haunted the book since it was first published, strikes me as absurd. To be sure, Gypsy had help. George Davis edited her. Lee Wright sent her pages of detailed notes and set her up with Craig Rice, the Chicago reporter and mystery writer. She was no Proust. But the "Striptease Intellectual" is more than a mass culture fantasy. Besides her radio and TV charisma, Gypsy did things in private that suggest an attention to literature more enduring than that of most other stars I can think of, and certainly more enduring than most strippers I've read about before or since. Throughout her life Gypsy snipped "Great Minds"— a newspaper feature describing intellectual giants's lives—and saved them with the idea of interpolating them in her numbers. A great synthesizer, she coined aphorisms such as "God is love, but get it in writing."

But most of all, Gypsy wrote about herself at a time when few women entertainers—few women of any kind—were doing so. Titled "Christmas on the Keith Family Circuit," her first autobiographical piece appeared in *Harper's Bazaar* the same year her book was published. From that moment she regarded her book's heroine "Gypsy" as an extension of her onstage persona. Sometime after the fictional character she created in *The G-String Murders* eclipsed the renown of the one she played onstage, a reporter asked if she would star in the Broadway adaptation of the novel. She responded: "I'd be a dope to play for $350 a week the part of a Chicago stripteaser when I can *be* the Chicago stripper for $2000."

A force in Gypsy's transformation from Queen of Striptease to Striptease Intellectual was women. Though in burlesque in the early 1930s she had appealed to "bald head" burlesque goers, gay men, the intelligentsia and the dates they dragged along, a few members of the Algonquin Round Table, and prostitutes, once she crossed over to the Follies the number of middle-class women in her fan pool increased. These women followed Gypsy to the stage door, demanded her autograph, and critiqued her costumes and furs. Gypsy always liked to lead her audiences to believe that these women scorned her, but the truth was that some of them saw her as an ideal. After the publication of Gypsy's novel, photos of *G-String Murders* signings show lines of women snaking out the door and into the street.

In Hollywood directors were more interested in the Queen of Striptease than ever, but only if her story got a fairytale ending. Released in January 1942, the Billy Wilder/Howard Hawks film

Ball of Fire is commonly understood to be based on *Snow White and the Seven Dwarves*. But the film also domesticates the street-wise stripper. Wilder pits Barbara Stanwyck (Sugarpuss O'Shea) against Gary Cooper (a Mencken-type figure researching American slang) in a Pygmalion story sentimentalizing Gypsy's rise to fame. The "stripteaser's education" inverts Gypsy's—Cooper is the intellectual here—although Stanwyck does teach him a thing or two about sex. The story ends happily ever after.

A Palace for the Striptease Intellectual

If *G-String* established Gypsy as an author, it also brought her real financial success. From 1930 to 1940 the stripper had lived at four New York addresses that roughly map her social peregrinations: Rego Park; East Thirty-sixth Street, north of Gramercy Park; a Fifty-seventh Street railroad flat; and Seven Middagh Street in Brooklyn.

With the money Gypsy made from *The G-String Murders*, she bought the four-story "Rutherford Palace" at 151 (now 153) East Sixty-third Street in New York. Named after Barbara Rutherford, Cornelius Vanderbilt's granddaughter, the building was erected in 1919. Gypsy decorated the rooms with homey touches such as Gibson girl drawings, a Bouguereau oil, a present from Mike Todd, and her own signature touches such as a mink toilet seat cover. She put living room chairs she had re-covered with her own needle-point designs on top of the elegant marble floor and scattered plastic and ceramic cherubs around. She also hung her framed tattoo collection on the wall and maintained a collection of rare trees. Reporters noted the mansion's lavishness and Gypsy's bedroom in particular, characterizing it as "prim," despite plush mauve velvet armchairs and the ornate oak bed that once belonged to President William Henry Harrison. Photographers posed Gypsy in profile against her fine china or in her library wearing a pink taffeta Charles James "tree gown," so called for the bouffant skirt that spread out around her ankles like the roots of a banyan tree. The backdrop—her paintings and sculpture, and a zebra-skin rug inspired by the ones on the banquettes at El Morocco—projected wealth. She now lived the life she had invented.

Although Sixty-third Street between Third and Lexington Avenues was home to many New York City notables, it became known as "the Gypsy Rose Lee block." The neighbors' responses to Gypsy's plan to widen the house sound as though she is bumping them offstage.

From Star and Garter to Self-portrait and Max Ernst

In 1942 three men from Peoria wired the army to say that they would like to join the Office of Civilian Defense. Since they were not Gypsy Rose Lee, they wondered, was that possible? "Is this a war or a burlesque show?" they asked. The press got hold of their wire and published it as news. If Gypsy had seen the wire, she might have answered, "Both." But she was too busy recycling her number from the mid-1930s to worry about critics. A photo from a performance she gave that year at the Music Box Theatre is nearly identical to ones from the Irving Place in the mid-1930s: at the penultimate moment of her act, her blouse slides off her shoulder, she holds her strip skirt in front of her, and she covers one breast with her hand as she looks away from the camera.

In Gypsy's defense, it is difficult to escape the banality of striptease. Everyone looks the same, more or less, when they take off their clothes. Striptease is not an art form, or at least not in the sense that painting is. Or at the very least we perceive nakedness as original at some times and pornographic at others. The closest we get to thinking about striptease as an original art is when someone else has made the naked woman into a nude and she has been hung in a museum. If the woman is undressing onstage, and if she is to be considered artistic, her props must be so outrageous and her jokes so funny as to set her apart from all other imitations. Gypsy needed to come up with something new to indicate that undressing was a wartime original. She needed a comeback vehicle that would please a publicity-wary country immersed in a European war.

Once again Mike Todd rescued her—or was it the other way around? Todd was producing an old-fashioned revue, *Star and Garter*, and Gypsy would star. The revue opened in June as an exercise in nostalgia, a love letter to a more innocent time—Todd

Gypsy Rose Lee in *Star and Garter,* 1942. Billy Rose Theatre Division, The New York Public Library for the Performing Arts, Astor, Lenox and Tilden Foundations

borrowed the revue's name itself from a turn-of-the-century burlesque show. When a backer withdrew, Gypsy stepped in. As part of the agreement, the show initially was to be called "The Gypsy Rose Lee Follies." With music by Harold Rome and the Ray Sinatra Orchestra, *Star and Garter* presented a naughty lineup of vaudeville acts and stripteases, but the apotheosis of the evening was "I Can't Strip to Brahms," Gypsy's updated version of her 1936 number "Stripteaser's Education."

"Brahms" differed from "Stripteaser" in at least one way. Whereas "Stripteaser" describes Gypsy's "elite" childhood, "Brahms" tells of her "failures" to clean up burlesque. If "Stripteaser" is about what Gypsy was, Brahms is about what she was not. The two songs both begin with stanzas about her fake past performing at the opera and the ballet, but by the second stanza "Brahms" has given up any pretense of gentility. Instead, the song uses music to explain why Gypsy cannot make striptease respectable. So rarified is this song's narrator that, as she strips, the arrangements quote from the composers that she "cannot" strip to. She sings that she "can't do the bumps to Puccini. . . . I could never take a corset off to the music of Rimsky-Korsakov. . . . Gawd knows I would play to an empty house if I had to strip to the music of Johann Strauss." (In the LP Gypsy added sound effects, such as clinking armor, to show how difficult it was to take it off to Wagner. After a few stanzas, the music speeds up and a big band sound takes over, allowing that strip tease without classical music might be modern and fun.) Gypsy mocks "high-brow culture" and suggests that, though she can now afford champagne and caviar, she prefers ordinary American fare. But her costumes were hardly ordinary. In *Star and Garter*, more than in any previous spectacle, she abandoned the Victorian for the circus, nostalgia for fantasy.

Offstage, back in the 1930s Gypsy had gone to a lot of trouble to dress well, ordering her clothes from Paris. When the war made such extravagance impossible, she commissioned Hollywood designer Edith Head, ballet costumier Karinska, or her old friend Pavel Tchelitchew. Mr. John made some of her hats. In an era when many American women wore extravagant hats, Gypsy went out of her way to outdo them. Charles James—the American couturier worn by Mrs. Vincent Astor and Diana Vreeland—contributed to Gypsy's style, designing the "New Look," suits and sculpted ball gowns that offset her onstage pizzazz with timeless elegance.

At the same time, Gypsy also began to steal the designs of couturiers she adored. But this was not simply a case of sartorial plagiarism. She copied with impunity the dresses and suits James (and others) had made for London or New York or Hollywood royalty. Besides her desire to save money, this impulse reveals Gypsy's wish—was it by this time a perversion?—both to invent herself and to fit in. Mixing carnival and haute couture in differing proportions, according to the time, the place, and the venue, increased her appeal to the women in her audience.

If *Star and Garter* also gave Gypsy a wide range of comic and erotic roles, a good number of these roles presented her as fantastical. In one number she glided onstage in an outfit, designed by Karinska, that included three starched petticoats and crocheted pasties in the shape of flowers. If she touched them they unraveled. For "The Girl on the Police Gazette," an Irving Berlin number from the film *On the Avenue*. Gypsy adorned herself in a full net body stocking with a silver spangled bikini and silver epaulets. The costume looks like a silver birdcage. A silver jewel is stuck in her belly button. An enormous tulle train drags behind her, and on her head rests a wide feathered hat. She carries a wand punctuated with a large star. The baroque set for this number was composed of a scrim with the logo from the *National Police Gazette*, the 1890s pink tabloid devoted to sports and burlesque. Reverting to luxury (her "real" self) for the finale, Gypsy wore a Charles James evening gown the designer called "La Sirene." Compared to Georgia Sothern—the stripper whom Todd hired to take it off to "Hold That Tiger"—Gypsy was positively demure.

Star and Garter revived critics' accusations that Gypsy's class act betrayed her humble burlesque origins. That *Star and Garter* tickets cost $4.40 inspired Damon Runyon to complain in his syndicated column that "the poor man has been robbed" by striptease's gentrification. Gypsy, Runyon argued, had abandoned the working man who supported her before anyone else did.

After *Star and Garter* Gypsy performed "Stripteaser's Education" or "I Can't Strip to Brahms" for the next two decades, tweaking them only for fashion's sake by adding the obligatory coda about her success or a line acknowledging rock and roll. The rags-to-riches tale of a stripper who loved to read, listen to classical music, and think about sex still interested Americans.

Gypsy's offstage life moved to the center. While secretly carrying on with Todd in the summer of 1942, she married Alexander "Bill" Kirkland, who was then starring on Broadway in the comedy *Junior Miss*. A successful Hollywood actor during the early 1930s as well as a member of the Group Theatre, Kirkland also happened to be gay. Peggy Guggenheim, who attended the wedding, wrote that Kirkland was "hardly suitable as a husband." But was Gypsy a suitable bride? She scheduled the ceremony at midnight in Highland Mills to give Mike Todd more time to rush in and rescue her from this marriage. She wore a black dress designed by Pavel Tchelitchew. Grapes hung in her hair.

Her costume was not the only thing that made the wedding seem like a burlesque show. There was also the cast: literati and famous guests from the showbiz and art worlds. Max Ernst was there, as was Gil Maison, the circus performer who played the shill when Gypsy took off her clothes onstage. Carl Van Doren, who had introduced the couple, was the best man. A chimpanzee was the ring bearer. *Life* magazine did a photo spread on the wedding, and some of the smaller papers announced that the real event was the reconciliation between Gypsy and Rose, the mother-daughter sideshow.

If weddings can auger a marriage's future, this one suggested disaster. The chimp peed on Kirkland. A photo in which the groom is slipping the ring on Gypsy's finger shows the star gazing at her hand as though posing in a hand cream ad. Todd never showed up. Kirkland and Gypsy took a one-day honeymoon. The marriage cracked into an annulment after three months.

Published that fall, Gypsy's second thriller, *Mother Finds a Body*, also cracked. Set mostly in Ysleta, a Texas border town, the novel is best read as a psychological working out of the events of 1937, when Rose's weird behavior reached its apotheosis. The heroine, Gypsy Rose Lee, skips through dope fiends, burlesque, and dead bodies for over three hundred pages before helping to solve the murders. The most amusing scenes describe stripteases or costumes, or relate anecdotes about "Evangie," the Rose character. The *New York Times* wrote that "we are glad to note that Gypsy Rose Lee does not lean quite so heavily on vulgarity as she did in *The G-String Murders*."

Perhaps the lukewarm critical reception to *Mother Finds a Body* inspired Gypsy to seek a new arena to conquer as she had done in the 1930s. Or perhaps she wanted to spend money conspicuously. Either way, she began to dabble in the art world; bidding on paintings by Degas and Dufy at Sotheby's, she bought them as an investment. At first she harbored the idea that having owned these paintings would cause their value to appreciate, but just as she genuinely loved books so she grew to genuinely love art and artists. Her taste ranged from the great moderns to her great friends: O'Keeffe, Ernst, Miró, Chagall, Cocteau, Picasso, Fannie Brice, and Marcel Vertes all hung on her walls. Her taste was not, as Todd's biographer Art Cohn claims, vulgar. When Mike Todd offered her a choice of three paintings, she chose a large female nude by Bouguereau, the academic French painter. Cohn makes a point of saying that the other two paintings were by Gauguin and Rousseau, but rather than proving her bad taste this demonstrates her interest in extending her persona into a brand. She also owned a collection of Charles Dana Gibson plates.

Just as reading led to writing, and wearing clothes led to making them, collecting led to creating art that puzzled out her identity. Her chosen genre was the collage; *Self-portrait* articulates the failure of Gypsy's cobbled-together selves to cohere. In a shadow box, she tops her *Star and Garter*–costumed body with a photo of a dog's head. A photo of a woman's body in a Victorian bathing suit is stuck on another head shot. A newspaper photo of her face above Walter Winchell's name suggests that her mind and her dreams could meet only under the sign of publicity. All of the figures float above seashells at the bottom of the frame. Maybe Gypsy meant *Self-portrait* to repeat the joke she had played as the Queen of Striptease, when she pretended to be an American aristocrat. It pops up in the background of a photo in which Gypsy is posed in Grecian robes, in profile, in front of her art collection.

Self-portrait was not just a vanity project. It asked viewers: where is the striptease? In January of 1943 it, along with another of Gypsy's works, hung in the "Exhibition of 31 Women," the "fantastical" art exhibit housed in Peggy Guggenheim's new gallery, "Art of This Century," on West Fifty-seventh Street. The jury for this famous exhibit included Marcel Duchamp, Ernst, and André Breton. Djuna Barnes showed in it as did Dorothea Tanning, Meret Oppenheim, Frieda Kahlo, and Louise Nevelson. (According to John Cage, Joseph Cornell "idolized" Gypsy, whom he met after she bought one of his works.)

Like her stripping, her acting, and her writing, Gypsy's collage invited ridicule. One reader wrote to the *New York Times* art critic, "If she's an artist, I'll send you a pound of coffee." But the collage appeared, along with the rest of the exhibit, in the lavish surrealist periodical *VVV*, which sculptor David Hare edited that year. On the same page was a photo of her in her *Star and Garter* costume and a portrait she commissioned Ernst to paint of her, as if by piecing together different images one could find the real person, or at least *a* real person.

Max Ernst's portrait of Gypsy is unlike any other existing image of her. You might say that it creates a separate illusion—the Gypsy who might have been. More mermaid or ghost than human, Ernst's *Gypsy*, a phantasmagoric creature covered with either feathers or scales, floats through macabre, mossy landscapes. Ernst divorces Gypsy from her burlesque past and striptease and sends her into flight like the Loplops—the made-up birds whose identities he adopted and who appear in so much of his prewar work. These elements' absence is itself noteworthy in that without them Gypsy gets transformed into a supernatural being.

"Doing a Striptease in Which She Doesn't Take Off a Thing"

In the real world, Gypsy's romance with Todd dragged on. Although he had let her marry another man, he continued to woo her. "I miss you so don't marry any actors, not even a butcher," read one telegram, dated 1943, months after her wedding, referring to the "candy butcher"—the vendor who strolled up and down the aisles at the burlesque theater selling hotdogs, chocolate, and racy picture books. But whether she was a ghost or a mermaid, an intellectual or a piece of Americana, in love with an actor or a butcher, one thing was certain: Gypsy was no longer a sex symbol. In a March 1943 article she wrote for *Mademoiselle* titled "What's New in War Wolves," she complains about her transformation from sex object to household name. Although she describes herself as wearing a skin-tight, red-sequined dress slit up to her thigh, she wrote that the sexy merchant marines that come to see her escort Vassar grads as opposed to Ladies of the Night. The punch line involves a merchant marine introducing Gypsy to his mother.

Gypsy's success in the 1940s contains many of these "I used to be a sex symbol" comic bits. The naughty self that she had constructed had gotten her to Hollywood and Broadway, but, upon her arrival those places divested her of her sex appeal. To succeed she would have had to tone it down. So when the film version of *The G-String Murders* was released in the spring of 1943, the first American movie written by and about a stripper lacked a striptease. During the production process Gypsy even coached director Hunt Stromberg on how the character based on her could strip "without actually doing so."

A movie that teased about a strip without a strip: that was typical Hollywood sleight of hand. The *New York Times* criticized *The G-String Murders*—which the studio retitled *Lady of Burlesque*—for lacking glamour, then turned around to say that burlesque by its very nature was unglamorous. *Lady of Burlesque* grossed $1.85 million on a promise to give audiences a glimpse of Gypsy's backstage life and her striptease. But it never delivered. Instead of answering the question Gypsy had asked a decade earlier—were women who took off their clothes onstage thinking about sex?—as the *New York Times* noted, in *Lady of Burlesque* Barbara Stanwyck "threatens to revolutionize the entire undress industry with a striptease in which she doesn't take off a thing."

This was not quite the situation in the movie version of *Stage Door Canteen*, but it was close. A legendary war effort, featuring such stars as Tallulah Bankhead, Katharine Cornell, Katharine

Hepburn, Harpo Marx, and George Raft as well as Gypsy, *Stage Door Canteen* was released in the summer of 1943 after a successful theatrical run. Produced by Sol Lesser, the film is a patriotic love story between a soldier and a hostess as well as a star-studded gala. It also contains the only existing film version of Gypsy's striptease, which ensured that it would receive a "B" rating from the Legion of Decency. The striptease begins with the camera panning the crowd, which is full of soldiers and their girlfriends. Everyone is having a good time. The emcee introduces Gypsy, "who went from without rags to riches." A laugh track responds. The star enters, wearing one of her archetypal costumes: the picture hat, the voluminous skirt with a Harlequin pattern; the blouse with Leg of Mutton sleeves. She has threaded rags through her hair, tying it in two Pippi Longstocking braids. She looms above the soldiers, who are gathered around her like children waiting for their bedtime story.

And what a bedtime story it is. Gypsy begins to recite her number, pressing her palms in front of her like a nun. Using her fingers she ticks off all the things she is not thinking. A minute goes by and she has not removed a stitch of clothing. She begins to unbutton her blouse and unties the ribbon around her neck. She flashes her clavicle. She cocks her head and raises her skirt to her thighs. She takes off her garter and, bending from the waist, unrolls her stocking, teasing the soldiers with her white garter belt. Continuing her patter, Gypsy removes her hat, rolls up her sleeve, and flashes her forearm. She takes off her petticoat and throws it over one of the soldiers' heads. Like a ballerina on top of a music box when the music stops, she ends the striptease with a funny little curtsy. But before she can exit another solider shouts: "Take off what you did in *Star and Garter*," and Gypsy replies, "Take that off, boys? I'll catch cold!" To make up for saying no, as she exits she tosses her garter into the audience. A fight breaks out.

Besides prolonging the fantasy that Gypsy's act could incite a riot among the troops, what emerges out of *Stage Door Canteen* is that she is hiding her real striptease from the camera. That would take place elsewhere, behind closed doors and for a private audience. In the hall of mirrors world of American popular entertainment, there is always time for one more imitation, one more striptease. No one ever gets to see anything real.

When a new round of imitations appeared, it was more burlesque-y than any prior one. In the summer of 1943 the film version of Irving Berlin's musical revue *This Is the Army* includes a drag parody of Gypsy in *Stage Door Canteen*. Berlin's patriotic tale of former showmen putting on a show to raise morale made hundreds of thousands of dollars for the war effort. After opening on Broadway during the previous summer, it toured the country and then the world. Berlin celebrated every genre of entertainment and every soldier in the armed forces. But Julie Oshins's impersonation of Gypsy—mincing across the stage in a ruffled gown and a garden hat—was extraordinary. As with *Lady of Burlesque*, reviewers raved. But this time the imposter was a female impersonator, and reviewers commented that a man could do a better striptease than the striptease original herself. The *New York Times* wrote: "The Great Private Oshins out-Gypsys Gypsy."

So when *The Naked Genius*, the Striptease Intellectual's second play, opened on Broadway in the fall of 1943, it never stood a chance. A woman whose striptease could be outdone by that of a soldier dressed as a stripper could not possibly be a writer. Anyway, by the time it reached the Plymouth Theatre, *The Naked Genius* had a tormented history. In 1942 Gypsy had begun to work on the script, first called *The Ghost in the Woodpile*. Next it became *The Seven Year Cycle* as an homage to astrological cycles. Finally Mike Todd, who was producing, insisted that the word "naked" appear in the title. When *The Naked Genius* picks up Gypsy's story after her success with *G-String Murders*, it casts her as a fake. Stripper Honey Bee Carroll pens a well-received book and almost marries the publisher's handsome son, but then, like some of the heroines Gypsy played in the late 1930s, she dumps the literary guy and returns to "her place" on the burlesque stage. *The Naked Genius* contains some good one-liners defending Gypsy's career as well as a wedding lampooning her real one to Alexander Kirkland a year earlier:

"Ironic isn't it . . . I write a best seller so I can get two thousand a week in a burlesque house in Philadelphia?"

(About the novel Honey Bee has published) "It wasn't a gimmick . . . I had something to say and I said it."

"Every time I try to get out of burlesque . . . try to do something different, it turns out to be a gimmick."

Gypsy's co-writer, the playwright and script doctor George S. Kaufman, was so sure that *The Naked Genius* would bomb that he famously asked Mike Todd, the producer, to change his credit on the show to Jed Harris (whom he despised). Having managed to make *Naked Genius* the first play to be sold to Hollywood (for $350,000) while still in rehearsal, Todd refused. (The play had to run for three weeks for him to get his fee.) New Yorkers were buying tickets, and journalists were covering the backstage drama. What else could a producer want? Todd did not care whether critics panned the show in out-of-town tryouts. "No one expected her to write a first class drama. No one expected her to miss the bus by half a block," the *Boston Post* critic wrote.

Todd's solution? To make girlfriend Joan Blondell, a chorus girl whom he had cast, more like Gypsy herself. When *The Naked Genius* moved to New York, he recostumed Blondell in a "diaphanous negligee" and gave her a powder puff to hold. He added a waterfall to the set and monkeys to the cast. Nothing helped. The *New York Times* called the show "a polite bore" and marveled at its "love story that was practically girlish in its routine." Despite Todd's schemes—or perhaps because of them—*The Naked Genius* fared only slightly better in its movie incarnation, *Doll Face*. "With all due respect to Miss Hovick, her talents have been better demonstrated otherwise," wrote Bosley Crowther in the *New York Times*.

But *The Naked Genius* (and *Mother Finds a Body*) may also have failed for other reasons. As Americans became more deeply involved in World War II, they held tight to the view that a stripper who pretended to be a writer was not a suitable icon. (No matter that Gypsy herself went overboard to help out in the war effort: "You've got to show the boys what they're fighting for," she told Hedda Hopper that year.) It is also possible that Gypsy was blocked. Maybe she needed a Seven Middagh Street to inspire her, or perhaps she was too mired in despair over Mike Todd's affair with Joan Blondell to write anything good. (Some articles published at around the time of *The Naked Genius*'s Pittsburgh tryout quote Gypsy as saying that a movie star could not play a stripper—a charge she denied in a letter to Todd.)

Gypsy's editor, Lee Wright, blamed "the boys"—by which she meant Kaufman and Todd—for "mashing" *Naked Genius* into "a pulp." Gypsy herself (whom Todd had banned from rehearsal) pleaded: "You say you can razzle dazzle it . . . can you blame me for wishing that the play should stand on its own without a razzle dazzle?" After *The Naked Genius*, Gypsy wrote one more autobiographical play, *The World on a String*, which crackles. But it never got produced. She stayed away from Broadway for ten years.

I have another theory about Gypsy's uneven literary output in the 1940s. Because *Mother Finds a Body* and *The Naked Genius* failed to sing songs about the halcyon past, the public could not interpret them as fables. Both works told stories too close to the present to capture the popular imagination. While the American public is willing to suspend disbelief about a recycled fiction set once upon a time, it is less willing when that story takes place now. It is no accident that Gypsy would publish her next hit in 1957, when enough time had elapsed for her to draw on American nostalgia for the Jazz Age.

The idea that Gypsy was a fake continued to haunt her. In January of 1943 Dorothy Wheelock, a former *Harper's Bazaar* editor, sued Gypsy for $5,000 and half the royalties for her work on *The G-String Murders* three years earlier. Wheelock charged that not only had she collaborated with the stripper, she had connected her with Simon and Schuster, which published *The G-String Murders*. Gypsy countered that the editor may have written "a sample book," but that book was not *G-String*. She settled the lawsuit out of court, but the press had a field day with these accusations.

Shortly after the lawsuit Gypsy managed to both "out-Gypsy" her imitators and prove herself to be the genuine article by writing a book in what today has become our most discredited literary form: the memoir. Gypsy had been publishing autobiographical pieces since the winter after *The G-String Murders* appeared. But in the spring of 1943 she placed the first of three of these pieces, all of which were about her hard knock childhood in Harold Ross's *New Yorker.* The other two would appear before the end of the year. "Mothers and the Knights of Pythias"; "Mother and the Man Named Gordon"; and "Just Like Children Leading Normal Lives," established her story and cemented her reputation as a writer.

In the late 1930s and early 1940s Ross was publishing whimsical profiles by and about celebrities and eccentrics. But for the *New Yorker* to publish a stripper's "real" stories—written by that stripper—was unprecedented. As for Gypsy, selling stories about her nightmarish childhood and her career choice to the *New Yorker* gained her the cachet and credibility that, until that moment, she had grasped only in flashes. After that, she never hesitated to broadcast her authentic authorial pain. "Anyone who writes for the *New Yorker* gets a neurotic stomach. Mine is shot to hell," she told a reporter while she was laboring over the first of these pieces.

Beyond Gypsy's stomach, at a time when Freud was in vogue, the memoirs provided an explanation for armchair psychologists trying to understand how she came to perform a striptease: Rose. Were Gypsy's *New Yorker* stories true? Does it matter? Would it matter now? Tossing truth with nontruth was not unique to Gypsy, or even to the Hovicks: but Gypsy excelled at it.

Furious over Gypsy's *New Yorker* version of their life, Rose submitted her own manuscript to Simon and Schuster, which, according to the columnist Hedda Hopper, if published would compel Gypsy to sue. Only one piece of Rose's version of Gypsy's story ever got published, albeit in a venue that was several notches below the *New Yorker.* The *New York Journal American* ran "Gypsy's Growing Pains," invoking Gypsy's teen weight problem and her topless audition, at age fifteen, for Jazz Age porn king Earl Carroll.

In the spring of 1944, while making *Belle of the Yukon,* the first film Gypsy performed in under her own name, she encountered the director Otto Preminger at the Beverly Hills home of Elsie de Wolfe Mendl, the actress, gay interior decorator, and socialite, whom she had known since the 1930s. Gypsy and Kirkland had finally gotten around to divorcing. The then-married Preminger had directed the psychological thriller *Laura* to much acclaim the previous year. Film critics write about the archetypal European director as a rake, as someone who ignored social niceties and taboos both on screen and in his personal life. In the 1950s he would become involved with Dorothy Dandridge.

As recounted by Erik, the relationship between his mother and Preminger, which took place in March of that year, sounds less like a white-hot passion than it does cozy domesticity. "She used to make dinners for me on a little hot plate," Preminger told his son in 1970. "One day I phoned her and the studio told me she had gone back to New York," he said. But then, as Erik tells it, Preminger plus Gypsy equaled a family, Gypsy style. The next time Preminger called, Gypsy was in the hospital. Erik had been born. According to Erik, on her deathbed Gypsy told her son that she wanted it that way.

D-Day brought with it economic prosperity and a sense of well-being, especially in New York. New ways of stirring high and low art emerged, and Gypsy's act—fresh and literate before the war—now seemed even less so. The Broadway musical *On the Town* provided a more modern take on striptease, alluding to it as though it were a corrupted dream and not a critique of the distribution of wealth or a measure of anyone's morality.

Hollywood remained stuck in the Paleolithic era. When *Belle of the Yukon* was released at the end of 1944, the former Queen of Striptease did not strip. "This is a period picture," Gypsy informed reporters who asked about it. Tinseltown's reluctance to let Gypsy take off her clothes was not that surprising. One of its strategies is to toss sirens into the past so that audiences can ogle them and still be virtuous. Playing Belle de Valle, the head of a troupe of showgirls, the ex-girlfriend of Randolph Scott and the rival of Dinah Shore, Gypsy resembles Mae West in that star's later roles. There is something ossified about her. Gypsy gets in some good lines, such as, when advising Shore about how to deal with a broken heart: "Time. Diamond bracelets speed things along. A new hat. The best thing's to get mad. Break something. Over the guy's head, if possible." But "her usual earthiness and humor are buried under a ton of plumes, big hats, and bustles," the *New York Times* complained.

The film's real star is Gypsy's costumes. Swaddled in hues of brown, gray, and white, the other actors fade next to Gypsy, whose dresses, designed by Don Loper, are larger and more vivid than anything else on-screen: a forest-colored scroll-shaped velvet hat topped with a bunch of fake violets; a strapless magenta taffeta gown with a train; a mint tulle negligee festooned with an enormous tulle rose on one shoulder; a gold lame evening dress trimmed in fur. Striding down Main Street next to Randolph Scott, dog under her arm, Gypsy and her clothes crackle. Hopper's column published the dollar values of Gypsy's costumes so that filmgoers could know that the woman who became famous taking it off would now spare no expense to get dressed.

With the end of the war came American prosperity but not a family cease-fire. Rose accelerated her pleas that her daughter stop telling tales about her. "Can't you write about other people?" she asked. Gypsy could not. She was supporting Aunt Belle and Big Lady. The Gypsy Rose Lee Papers family correspondence folders from the mid-1940s are full of demands for money forwarded to Gypsy from the Welfare Office in Seattle, from doctors, from dentists. Gypsy sometimes paid, but by D-Day she refused, via lawyers, to allow her family to hold her hostage for telling the truth. When, in 1945, the prodigal daughter visited what remained of the Hovicks in Seattle for the first time, she brought them red shoes and black lace strip panties. In letters recounting this visit to Rose, Aunt Belle and Big Lady complain that Gypsy is nice to them only when newspaper reporters are around.

"Out-Gypsying" Gypsy once again picked up, as though the postwar generation needed to exert its own efforts to strip the veneer from Gypsy's unsettling striptease. In 1946 future novelist Jacqueline Susann starred as "ladylike" stripper Fudge Farrell in a touring production of Charles Raddock's play *Between the Covers*, which the author was inspired to write after Gypsy's publisher rejected his book. Thriller writer Craig Rice sent Gypsy a telegram: "current time magazine credits me with having written mother finds a body. I wish I had. I have sent them and [*sic*] indignant message regarding the error and hope you will do the same."

FIVE

Selling Striptease

Despite the postwar generation's expansive flair, at times a Victorian prudishness surged. At Christmas 1948 Gypsy performed on a live CBS television variety show from Madison Square Garden. Everything went smoothly as a parade of stars did their numbers. But the minute Gypsy touched her shoulder strap, announcing that she intended to do "Psychology of a Stripteaser," as *Time* magazine then called it, wavy gray lines appeared and "startled televiewers found themselves staring at nothing but the initials CBS, while in the background, Gypsy's voice trilled on, and enthusiastic Air Force veterans shouted the traditional 'Take it off! Take it off!'"

At first CBS denied that it had censored the program. Finally, however, the network admitted that "there were no technical

Gypsy Rose Lee at the Royal American Carnival. Billy Rose Theatre
Division, The New York Public Library for the Performing Arts,
Astor, Lenox and Tilden Foundations

difficulties," and that executives had made a decision to protect
the American people from salacious images. Gypsy responded:
"It was nearly midnight. Surely the kiddies aren't watching at that
hour!" When asked why she wore such long gloves, she sent the
same message on Clifton Fadiman's long-running program, *This Is
Show Business:* "So I'd have something to take off on the show."

When, a year later, Gypsy "ran away" to join the carnival, she was responding to that prudishness. But her elopement also has a familiar ring, recalling previous ones with burlesque, the Follies, and Hollywood. Each time Gypsy's success depends on her rescuing a vanishing genre of popular entertainment. In the late 1940s the carnival, like burlesque in the 1930s, clung to any act that might draw crowds: girls; feats of strength, freaks, striptease sideshows. The Royal American Carnival was among the most successful. Run by Carl J. Sedermayr, it toured the West, the Midwest, and Canada.

Some carnival folks speculated that Gypsy's appearance in their midst announced her demise: "were she as high and wonderful, whats [*sic*] she joining a carnival for, is it the last straw?" the Monkey Girl asked Hedda Hopper after she ran a column about Gypsy and her new profession. It was, in the end, a personal decision. After Sedermayr hired Gypsy to do ten shows a day in towns like Davenport, Iowa, and Saint Louis, she saw it as a homecoming. She missed the smell of greasepaint. The honky-tonk and the glittering lights reminded her of her childhood. "I can hardly wait until I get back with the show," she wrote to Hopper. Gypsy would travel with the carnival for the next several years, polishing her nightclub act and developing her own touring company, the Royal American Beauties. (The carnival was also child-friendly and allowed her to keep Erik, then six, by her side.)

Gypsy loved going to a new midway every day and setting up a city of tents in an empty field. The carnival returned her to people that she liked the most: simple country folks. She wrote to Hopper: "in practically every exhibit the whole family works . . . babies and diapers all over the place." Far from New York, in a new town every night, Gypsy could recycle her act with impunity. Her name was in lights. Fans fought to buy tickets. During the Korean War crowds of thousands thronged to her shows.

Gypsy changed some aspects of her act, especially her costumes. In the late 1940s Charles James designed a Merry Widow for her carnival numbers. Her costumes now suggested an effort to revive the contrast between luxury and humor she had honored in the Depression: in the middle of the woods, in front of the Rolls, Gypsy and Les Girls pose as though they were stranded. A white mink stole slinks around Gypsy's arms, and the girls wear full net panties, gloves, and high heels. But the danger is not that they are lost: a blond holds a traffic sign that says, "Curves ahead."

If the carnival provided the perfect backdrop for "Psychology of the Striptease," the star for the first time in years launched some new numbers, like the "fairy godmother in a Cinderella striptease." Lecturing the audience about her profession's history, she borrowed from her Gay Nineties number from *Star and Garter* and did a "reverse" striptease, taking off pieces of her gown to dress four half-naked girls. But a *Life* magazine photo best captures her in this incarnation. She stands in front of a giant banner displaying her portrait, in which her expression is closer to an Old Testament grimace than anything recognizable as pleasure. The real Gypsy, smaller and more lithe, arms bare and holding on to the tent rope, is smiling.

While staging her own version of *On the Road*, Gypsy was transformed by the 1950s media into the epitome of the domestic, consumerist American woman. This was the age of Doris Day, Elizabeth Taylor, and the lifestyle that would be depicted in *The Feminine Mystique*. But like much image-making, the transformation contained more than a grain of truth. Gypsy had always been interested in the "womanly" arts. During her marriage to Bob Mizzy she cooked him "city chicken"—lamb chops and pork chops on a skewer. Her appointment books were filled with recipes. But in the conservative postwar era, a single mother—especially one who used to be a stripper—needed to take a more active interest in the womanly arts than the happily married homemaker, at least on the surface. A piece Gypsy wrote in 1944, titled "The Things I Want," listed "a husband, baby, and home" and then blamed her marriages' failure on her career.

Gypsy exploited her love of things domestic: she held a weekly quilting bee for actresses Faye Emerson, Hermione Gingold, June, and Celeste Holm, which Alfred Eisenstadt photographed for *Life* magazine. In 1948 she wrote the forward for her friend

Eliot Elisofon's cookbook, *Food Is a Four Letter Word.* Elsewhere she described herself as a "homebody," although the Gypsy Rose Lee–style homebody might have eluded the housewife in Peoria. Or perhaps Gypsy gave this housewife an ideal to aspire to. In an episode of Edward R. Murrow's television show *Person to Person* Gypsy entertains Murrow at home. Wearing one of her Charles James gowns, she flirts: "Why don't you come upstairs to my tackle box?"

Unlike Mae West, Gypsy never aspired to be a "sexagenarian." Gore Vidal's *Myra Breckinridge* was not for her. The plays she starred in during this era, many of which June directed, were homecomings, journeys down 1930s lane, comfort food for McCarthy-era America: she rewrote *The Naked Genius* for a production in Bermuda; she played Sylvia, the gossipy wife in a revival of Clare Booth Luce's play about female rivalry, *The Women*, in Syracuse, New York, and Norwich, Connecticut; she starred in Ben Hecht's *Twentieth Century* at the Palm Beach Playhouse, and in Anita Loos's *Darling, Darling*, an adaptation of a Parisian farce about two women who love the same man, at the Pocono Playhouse. Outside of Manhattan, and away from the carnivals, Gypsy evoked a Faustian bargain with her audience: if in the middle of the Cold War she could conjure a simpler time through costume, set, laughter, and sex, she would give back their youth.

But when Gypsy played Vegas she engineered a return to her

striptease self by way of Liberace: a dress from her carnival and nightclub act weighed ninety-seven pounds and dripped with layers of silver bugle beads. A silver lamé gown opened to reveal Capri pants, suggesting transvestism, or, at least, liberation from femininity. "Gypsy Rose Lee . . . is sufficiently sock marquee to put ropes up both shows nightly," *Variety* judged.

Even though she earned $10,000 a week in Vegas, Gypsy's fear of being penniless drove her to scrimp. Erik recounts that she once responded to his request for a new wardrobe by commenting that "Harry Truman could find time to rinse out his socks and underpants every night." Other saving measures included giving Erik the Depression-era suits of her Broadway show producer friend, Leonard Sillman, cooking on a hot plate while traveling instead of spending money on room service, and turning down the heat in her Sixty-third Street house to a point where her son complained about the cold.

But when it counted, Gypsy spent lavishly so that, despite hoarding until the musical bearing her name became her annuity, she was often living beyond her means. "When it counted" centered on Gypsy's image, whether that involved her two-tone Rolls Royce with a tea service and a crystal vase on the dashboard, her designer costumes and clothes, or her houses on the Upper East Side and in Beverly Hills.

But no investment could protect her from communist hunters. Because she had stripped for the Spanish Loyalists years earlier, in 1950 Gypsy's name made it into the anti-Communist pamphlet *Red Channels.* Along with Arthur Laurents, Lillian Hellman, Marc Blitzstein, Josh White, and other theater artists, actors, and intellectuals, Gypsy, *Red Channels* reported, was "a dear and close associate of the traitors to our country." The pamphlet cited as proof one speech Gypsy gave to the Hollywood Anti-Nazi League in 1941, as well as three mentions in Eugene Lyons's exposé book, *Red Decade*, which described her striptease performance for the Abraham Lincoln Brigade and called her a "political neophyte."

Gypsy was angry. She had already defended actress Jean Muir after McCarthyites had succeeded in getting television show sponsor General Foods Corporation to blacklist her. And the network supported Gypsy. When American Legionnaire Ed Clamage—a man whom Studs Terkel called "the Joe McCarthy of Chicago"—wired Robert Kintner, then president of ABC, to demand that Kintner cancel *What Makes You Tick?*, Gypsy's new radio talk show, Kintner replied with his own demand: where was proof? The only "proof" Clamage could offer was *Red Channels.*

Gypsy told *Time:* "Look at me—I haven't slept in four nights. I have a terrible case of laryngitis from screaming my innocence at people." To the allegations of "front" activity she repeated what she had said when the Dies Committee investigated her in 1938: "Should we wire our Congressman to investigate before we do a benefit performance? I'm not a Red and never have been." Eventually, Gypsy signed a document swearing to that effect.

After the Red Scare, Gypsy began appearing regularly on television. Unlike many former vaudeville and burlesque stars whom TV obliterated, her larger-than-life presence suited the golden age of talk. She emceed *What Makes You Tick* in 1950 and appeared on *Think Fast* and also on *What's My Line?*, where she was the mystery guest, whose identity the panelists had to guess while blindfolded.

Gypsy took up her most serious political cause in this era: the performers' union. In 1949, already one of a few women nominated to the national board of the American Guild of Variety Artists (AGVA), she became editor of the *AGVA News*. In her inaugural editor's letter, Gypsy wrote a manifesto exposing the appalling conditions burlesque performers had endured before the union. She recalled that, when she had tried to organize in 1935, Billy Minsky had told her that "no actor should join a union. It isn't artistic. Unions are for laborers, people who dig ditches. You're an artiste. You should have star dust in your eyes and music in your heart."

Gypsy spoke openly about burlesque troupers' hard lives in a way that her films, stage shows, and novels never had:

> seven days a week four shows a day, forty-five hours of
> rehearsals a week for fifteen dollars. No contracts, no secu-

rity bond, supply your own shoes and keep smiling. . . .
Who wants to know from stardust in your eyes when your
feet hurt? Twenty-five percent of our weekly salary was
paid to us in i.o.u's, but I used mine to plug up the rat holes
in the dressing room. That was in 1933. In 1934, a group
of burlesque actors formed the burlesque artist's association. Two months later the variety actors formed their
union, later to be known as the agva, and the first strong
union of vaudeville actors since the White Rats.

Gypsy goes on to recount how, although actors got fined for
refusing to play for "no money," she was one of the first to do so.
She expresses her commitment to making sure producers re-
spected actors "like people." Although she could neither stem
the corruption plaguing AGVA nor convince other performers
in the union that strippers were entertainers and not prostitutes,
during her short tenure there she demonstrated that she was on
the working person's side.

In 1948 Gypsy met Julio de Diego, a Latin artist who would
become her third husband, at a party she attended with the
Life photographer Eliot Elisofon. It was love at first sight. De
Diego remembered that "he met a beautiful girl whose black pet-
ticoat edged with red ribbon swirled at the bottom of her dress."
The couple settled into relative domesticity—which for Gypsy

meant traveling around the country in a trailer. De Diego painted a surrealist mural on the trailer walls: *What Are Your Dreams?* But ultimately, although the de Diegos enjoyed both each other's company and dreams, neither one could sustain marriage.

De Diego balked at being Mr. Gypsy Rose Lee. "I am not cut out to be a prince consort," he said, explaining why their marriage ended in divorce in 1955, after several years of separation. As with Kirkland, the seeds of discontent may have been planted on the wedding day. "It was a very beautiful occasion . . . it was the simplest wedding possible, only our party of four, the Fox Movietone news and the newspaper photographers," de Diego said. Still, it takes two to tangle. De Diego saw his wife less as a woman than as an embodiment of a surrealist ideal. A collage he did pasted headless photographs of Gypsy's torso atop images of her legs pinwheeling from her dress, as though she were a real-life incarnation of a Busby Berkley musical. Around the margins de Diego scrawled bits of celebrity-inspired graffiti. A poem he wrote about Gypsy ended with the lines that he had:

Strangled her
To shut off
Her torrent
of
verbal
abuse

Even after they divorced, though, de Diego and Gypsy corresponded for years. But romantically Gypsy was restless. She behaved—as she always had—in a way that came into vogue for women only in the 1960s. She once said that she supported polygamy, but at the very least she was suspicious of domesticity. "The first year of marriage you're exploring everything new together. The second year you're reliving the first year. The third year it's just plain normal married life: I never made it through that," she said.

Gypsy's most serious and enduring relationship was with her mother even though, for the last ten years of Rose's life, the two spoke only through lawyers. Gypsy paid many of her mother's bills as a bribe to keep Rose out of her life. In 1951, three years before Rose's death, she wrote: "Haven't heard anything from mother recently, thank God." After Rose died, Gypsy noted in the appointment book she was using as her journal: "Mother died at 6:30." It is easy to see her jottings' brevity as reflective of a chilled temper and attitude. But could it not also reflect implacability, the trouper's stoicism, her devotion to the show going on? A New Year's resolution that year was to "speak well of all or not speak." When Mike Todd, the love of her life, died tragically four years later, Gypsy was similarly terse. "Mike was killed in a plane [crash] at 4:30." (She did draw a box around the sentence.)

Gypsy had always promoted herself but since the late 1940s she had shifted her energy from the theater to advertising. This transformation from actress to saleswoman was hardly unheard of among female stars, but Gypsy's success importing her strip-tease persona to marketing reveals how hungry Americans were in this to talk about sex. She was a female Alfred Kinsey, pre-scribing for Americans a franker, more commercial idea of sex (as long as it wasn't too frank). Typical of her approach was her speech at the Formfit Merchandise Clinic in 1950. Introduced as a "posture expert," she cracked jokes and recommended that lin-gerie makers make dressing rooms more attractive.

"And what about wired brassieres?" she asked. "Some of them are so loaded that you have to join the pipe fitters union to wear it. I like a little more wire, sure, but not a cyclone fence."

In 1954, having befriended Colonel Elliott White Springs, the iconoclastic chairman of Springmaid Linens, Gypsy starred in an ad campaign for the company, the tagline: "You love those slow burning Springmaid sheets." The ad outraged Madison Av-enue. After that, Gypsy became the company's spokeswoman. In a second ad in the same campaign she lounged on a bed and swore that Springmaid Candycale sheets were her "favorite nite spot."

If only Gypsy's theatrical roles had gone so smoothly. Most stars flail around when the culture changes. Studio executives considered Katharine Hepburn box office poison until she triumphed in *The Philadelphia Story*. Frank Sinatra struggled after the war before trading ebullience for 1950s cool. When, in 1957, twenty years after Gypsy had replaced Merman in *DuBarry was a Lady*, she stepped into the lead role in *Happy Hunting*, something seemed wrong. Part of the awkwardness was the musical itself. Lindsay and Crouse wrote *Happy Hunting* for Merman, who referred to it as a "jeep among limousines." The plot is uninspired: Wealthy widow Liz Livingstone accompanies her daughter to Monaco, where she contrives to marry her off to a rich suitor. The team crammed the musical full of topical references.

But it wasn't just one bad play. The year Jack Kerouac wrote *On the Road* was the year Americans lost interest in Gypsy's sophisticated parody of striptease.

The Death of Striptease

Touring in Europe in the early 1950s, Gypsy got mixed reviews. In Sweden she wrote: "Audiences watch me with their mouths wide open, but not longing for me. After all, they seem to be saying, 'we show more than that on the beach,' and indeed, with nude sunbathing, they certainly do." After a 1951 London engagement, the *News Chronicle* damned her: "At one stage she has a singular lack of clothes and at the same time a singular lack of wit."

Americans were often more polite. But during the Cold War, the striptease as Gypsy had introduced it—a witty, sexy act—had vanished. Save for a few louche niteries on "Stripty-Second Street," Fiorello La Guardia had shut down burlesque in New York in 1939. A version of striptease flourished in Las Vegas, once the Minsky Brothers, the burlesque impresarios whom Justice Brennan had chased out of Newark, New Jersey, went west. Striptease staggered on in Atlantic City, Dallas, Los Angeles, Miami, and San Francisco, and at clubs like the Crazy Horse in Paris. But in New York the Minskys' petitions to bring back "clean" burlesque (and with it striptease) met with good-humored indifference. Also, by the early 1950s cities where burlesque striptease had staggered on during wartime razed the slums where these theaters sat. Rumors of burlesque's mob connections and of links between striptease and prostitution made it more marginal still.

Whatever striptease was in the 1950s, it was rarely funny. Gypsy leapt onto the scene when Hollywood honored screwball comics like Carole Lombard, Claudette Colbert, Jean Arthur, and Rosalind Russell. But by the 1940s, femmes fatales, pinup girls, and love goddesses had replaced these funny ladies as though, once the economy improved, no one wanted to see women laughing.

Thanks to years of suppression by the Hays Office, no burlesque striptease exists in a studio-made film. The advent of *Playboy* and other "pin up" magazines, as well as Alfred Kinsey's books on sex, diminished striptease's taboo by giving Americans access to the naked female body in ways that had hitherto been possible only at a burlesque show. Yet although *Playboy* founder Hugh Hefner initially ran photos of pinup girls and strippers in his pages, he considered striptease too old-fashioned to be of much interest; in any event, Gypsy by that time was too old for his pages.

After the war Americans preferred either Lili St. Cyr's ascetic lavish pantomime takeoffs or the avuncular sugar mama style of Blaze Starr. We were still a few years away from the moment when *Notes on Camp* would explain how to revive obsolete forms of culture by adding wit.

1957–59: Gypsys

When Gypsy published her autobiography, *Gypsy,* in 1957, it was not a new story. She had been teasing readers with it for over a decade the way she teased audiences by removing one item of clothing at a time and then vanishing before taking everything off, leaving the rest to the imagination. So when Erik says that his mother wrote *Gypsy* in nine months between starring in a revival of the Ben Hecht play *Twentieth Century* at the Palm Beach Playhouse and doing her striptease act at the Sans Souci Hotel in Miami Beach, what he is really saying is that she picked up her clothing from the stage and sewed it into an almost new dress.

Gypsy tells her story in flashback, beginning in 1957 and then jumping to her childhood. It tours her early days on the road, rambles through 1930s burlesque, and ends in 1936 with her tri-

Gypsy Rose Lee and Ethel Merman during rehearsal for *Gypsy*, 1959.
Billy Rose Theatre Division, The New York Public Library for the
Performing Arts, Astor, Lenox and Tilden Foundations.

umph in the Follies as she is en route to Hollywood. As with
G-String Murders, *Gypsy* pleased fans and alienated critics, who
used the book as an opportunity to deride striptease and the author's credentials. One reviewer found the book "depressing and
undependable." Others raised the old objection about Gypsy's
spurious literary claims. "This Stripper Can Write!" a headline proclaimed. Still others accused her of being mean. Allen

Churchill complained: "Her clever remarks have a raucous edge that rob[s] them of humor." When the *Chicago Tribune* serialized the book, some readers wrote in to say that the newspaper, celebrating a stripper's success, was doing the Devil's work. But Gypsy's memoir preceded a slew of female celebrity tell-alls that would appear in the next few years.

Broadway producer David Merrick bought the rights to *Gypsy*, and, after unsuccessfully wooing the lyricist/composer team of Betty Comden and Adolph Green, convinced the quartet of Arthur Laurents, Stephen Sondheim, Jule Styne, and Jerome Robbins to tackle the project. Set in the Jazz Age and the Depression, *Gypsy*, a *Musical Fable*, focuses on Mama Rose, the stage-door mother who flings her daughter into a life of undressing with all of the sentimentality of a spider devouring its young. Loud, ambitious, thwarted, and materialistic, Rose pushes June into a vaudeville career and thus drives her away. Vaudeville dies. In act 2, Rose tries to work her magic on the wallflower, Gypsy, who proceeds to both exceed and destroy the mother by becoming a stripper in the Ziegfeld Follies, the *American Idol* of its day.

As Laurents put it: "The story of a woman who became the striptease queen of America did not interest me." In 1957 what did interest Laurents and his collaborators, entwined in Cold War morality and their own *meshugas*, was Rose. The Sondheim-Laurents-Styne-Robbins *Gypsy* ends on Broadway, after the ugly duckling becomes the swan, when the Mean Queen "recognizes" her creation and regrets subsuming her own talents. Gypsy's journey from "Queen of Striptease" to "Striptease Intellectual" is less important than Rose's bitter, thwarted hopes. But she does accuse her daughter of being a fraud who "reads book reviews like they was books."

In 1959, when the musical premiered on Broadway, America's Most Famous Stripper was not concerned about whether it was documentary, fiction, or memoir. Gypsy saw *Gypsy* as (just) another vehicle with which to promote herself. Unlike June, who fought the musical's opening to try and get Sondheim and Co. to make her character more sympathetic, Gypsy didn't care how the boys presented her, so long as the show had her name on it and tickets got sold. Gypsy was thinking about what was to her a more central problem than the truth: the amount of exposure that was desirable. "I must not play Casa Cugat," she concluded in her journal, referring to the nightclub where she had agreed to headline at the time of the musical's opening. "It is wrong for me to be shaking the beads in a saloon while the 'myth' is on Broadway. The original must live up to the story."

But who was the original? Gypsy had answered Laurents's query about the genesis of her name with a classic evasion: "Oh darling, I've given so many versions, why don't you make up your own?" Her continuous voguing and teasing helped Gypsy keep much in her personal life private. Still, one of her most throwaway statements reveals much about her interior, the way the pins she tossed into the tuba in the 1930s revealed a lot about her act's intention. "I don't mind working awfully hard but I work hard to keep it light," she told a reporter in 1957.

Let Me Not Strip for You

In 1959 Merman made Rose, just like Brando had made Stanley Kowalski. Broadway's (and later Hollywood's) most flamboyant actresses and musical comedy divas—Rosalind Russell; Angela Lansbury; Tyne Daly; Bernadette Peters, Bette Midler, Patti LuPone— have really only ever been contenders. Yet whereas Rose conjured Merman, the ingénue evoked tabula rasa. Marilyn Monroe was never considered for the role of the young Gypsy. Sophia Loren, Jane Seymour, and Elizabeth Taylor were never dreamed about, and not just because they couldn't sing. The actresses who have played Rose's daughter are variations on the Audrey Hepburn theme: Sandra Church, Natalie Wood, Christine Ebersole.

Kenneth Tynan's *New Yorker* review of the Broadway premiere criticized Church as "too chaste in demeanor to reproduce the guileful, unhurried carnality with which the real Gypsy undressed." Arthur Laurents blamed Church for these qualities, but the young Gypsy's lack of va-va-voom was not solely the actress's fault. During the Cold War the idea that a woman would warm up to being a stripper would have been too daring for Broadway audiences to consider. This was not France, or even

Great Britain. It was the America of Saul Bellow, Norman Mailer, Phillip Roth, Che Guevara, Fidel Castro, Senator Joseph McCarthy, and Hugh Hefner. It was essentially a masculine rather than a feminine era, one where a stripper on the Broadway stage was most likely a sex kitten or a joke.

As for the sexy comic hijinks Gypsy embodied in real life, the musical boils them down to three numbers implying that allure cultivated between men and women while laughing was in and of itself a con. Gypsy herself said, as early as 1937, "You can't sell sex and humor at the same time." The number Gypsy became famous for in the 1930s was both smarter and more demure than "Let Me Entertain You," whose brashness epitomized the 1950s. "You Gotta Have a Gimmick" uncovers less about the "real" Gypsy than it does about Cold War ambivalence toward female carnality. Finally, the finale, "Rose's Turn," though not technically a striptease, forces the true star of the show to reveal the ambition and rage she had spent her entire life hiding.

During the musical's creation, Laurents and Robbins had tangled over how risqué Gypsy's act 2 striptease should be. In 1959, still a few years before the sexual revolution made onstage nudity chic, Laurents was leery of alienating his middle-class audience. As Deborah Jowitt tells it in her biography of Jerome Robbins,

Laurents wrote the choreographer a note to dissuade him from making the striptease too vulgar:

> We are all absolutely convinced that the moment she [Gypsy] steps out of the dress, she is cheapened and vulgarized. The audience does not want to see it. They want to see her tease and love her when she does. But the moment is vulgar, the rolling up in the curtain is vulgar—terribly so—the movement makes her cheap, common, ordinary—and hurts both Louise and Rose for the rest of the show. About the tease, she was always a lady. If you feel that she must be nude, please restrict to a flash when she is in the white furs. Perhaps if it is as though the furs were slipped back without her knowledge, and she pulls them back with a smile, that would be acceptable. . . . Please keep her a lady.

It is not known how Robbins replied. But Gypsy's striptease in the musical is all about her mother. "Mama, I'm pretty," is her famous line as she looks in the mirror right before she is about to take off her clothes. At first her mother eggs her on from backstage, shouting, "Sing out, Louise." Not too long after that, Gypsy begins to insert her own flirty touches. She designs her own risqué costumes. But if her striptease established her as "not" her mother, it never enters the world of adult sexuality.

My mother—who got me into this business—
(she is pulling up her dress)
always told me—make them beg for more.
And then don't give it to them.
(drops the dress)
But I'm not my mother.

Gypsy was not the only musical from this era using striptease to add texture. The year before *Gypsy* opened, Bob Fosse had choreographed the *Damn Yankees* number "Whatever Lola Wants" for Gwen Verdon and showed Lola stripping with verve. Verdon glides across the stage, shaking her body in a half-sexy, half-satiric number. Striptease for adults: now it caricatures desire, now it incarnates it.

Without the real Gypsy and her burlesque career, Fosse's striptease would never have appeared in a musical about baseball. Yet compared with Verdon's striptease, *Gypsy*'s look hokey. Only in the 1960s did the stripper as a character became erotic in the modern sense, as in Jane Fonda's space-age striptease in Roger Vadim's *Barbarella*.

Asked by a journalist about her mother on the eve of the musical's premiere, Gypsy responded, "I can't think of Rose as being dead." Neither could critics. When *Gypsy* opened on May 21, they fastened more on Rose's complexity than on Gypsy's striptease. Walter Kerr described her as a "mastodon"; Kenneth

Tynan compared her to "a nightmare incarnation of Mrs. Worthington," Noël Coward's stage-door mother, and *New York Times* theater critic Brooks Atkinson wrote that she was a "juggernaut."

California

Even after the musical, Gypsy dreamed of new ways to sell her story. In 1958 she had begun to compile "A Curious Evening with Gypsy Rose Lee" from movie clippings and stills, with the idea that she do a lecture tour and make a lot of money. There are no extant copies. But according to Erik, the history of his mother was also a history of the twentieth century, complete with newsreels and footage of sporting events. When Gypsy brought *Curious Evening* to New York in 1961, critics greeted her warmly. Taken by the merry-go-round of Gypsy's life, the jazz writer Whitney Balliett observed at the New York premiere, "Folklore doesn't become folklore all by itself." He added that Gypsy, in a tight V-necked black gown, white foxtail wrap, and gloves, was "pretty intact too." The *New York Times* agreed: "We love you, Gypsy."

Not everyone felt the same way—especially not the surviving family members. In 1959 June's first memoir, *Early Havoc*, appeared to correct Gypsy's whitewashed portrait of their mother and their childhood. The *New York Times* review compared the sisters to the Brontës. But Gypsy herself was more interested in real estate than in continuing the war-between-the-Hovicks over their past. The same year she toured *Curious Evening* she sold her New

York house and moved to 1240 Cerrocrest Drive in Beverly Hills, which she referred to as "Naked Acres," or "early Gloria Swanson." Originally owned by the Dohenys, the wealthy oil family, the house served as a different kind of stage. When Gypsy bought the Spanish-style villa overlooking Beverly Hills, Los Angeles, and Hollywood, she made it even more lavish than her New York home. The interior assimilated many of the different venues she had played on over the years, but mostly it evoked the carnival.

"It was like an Italian palazzo," said Barbara Preminger, Erik's former wife. Set on two acres, the palazzo boasted a swimming pool, a screening room, and a moat stocked with goldfish. Gypsy painted the drawing room walls green and the ceiling gold, which gave it an "unworldly" quality, according to social chronicler David Patrick Columbia, who visited the estate. The harp from *Three-penny Opera* sat in one corner. A portrait of Gypsy lounging on a re-camier hung above the real recamier. She had painted the dining room ceiling with a trompe l'oeil of blue sky and clouds. Less-public rooms, such as the kitchen, were less dramatic. That the press treated "Naked Acres" as camp—really the only picture of aging female Hollywood stars—failed to diminish its power.

After Gypsy's death, in 1971 Sotheby's would auction most of the house's furniture and objets. A short list of the museum-quality items includes: velvet and satin Pullman chairs; peacock fans; a parasol that used to belong to Sarah Bernhardt; and a pa-pier-mâché table with a mother-of-pearl model of the Windsor

Castle attached to it. Gypsy's G-strings were missing, but according to the *New York Times* a mink one turned up at a second auction held in 1979, where a London banker bought it. Convinced that Gypsy's ghost haunted the house, later owners had it torn down.

When *Gypsy* opened on Broadway, Gypsy was dating Billy Rose, who had fired her thirty years earlier. I do not think that this relationship was sexual, but even so it was the last time she would try to make a go of it with a man. In California Gypsy abandoned her romantic life for a domestic one, with her friends, her speaking engagements and her TV shows, interior decorating, and a menagerie of dogs, canaries, goldfish, peacocks, and the obligatory monkeys. Several photos from this era show the dogs and monkeys posed as people, wearing suits, riding bicycles, or holding barbells. Gypsy was not the first or only female star to keep a menagerie. Josephine Baker, Sarah Bernhardt, and Doris Day all had pets. When Mae West was making *I'm No Angel* in 1934, she traveled with a chimp. Fans expected female celebrities to keep animals and to dress them up as people, as either compensation for not having children (or not having enough of them) or proof of their primitive character. (Michael Jackson, after all, acquired a zoo.) In the vaudeville days the Hovicks had traveled with a chimp, a horned toad, dogs, a white rat named Molly, and a guinea pig named Sambo. When money was tight, they would sell the creatures. But at her California home Gypsy harbored only rare species, as if she were constructing her own

Gypsy Rose Lee feeding a puppy. Billy Rose Theatre Division, The New York Public Library for the Performing Arts, Astor, Lenox and Tilden Foundations

luxury ark. She turned one section of her house into an aviary and another into an aquarium. She began to breed the species of toy dogs known as Chinese Crested Hairless, joking that she had an affinity for them because they were "bare."

Gypsy referred to her animals as her "family." For an aging stripper to dress up monkeys and breed tiny dogs suggests nostalgia for her childhood on the road. It also evokes *Sunset Boulevard*. Still, Gypsy's journey to old age was smoother than that of other female stars because she had stopped insisting that audiences consider her a sex symbol decades earlier. Now even more like Garbo, Gypsy had always wanted to be alone (with pets) as though proving the cliché that, in our culture, to buy respite from the clamor you have to be famous.

Hollywood only offered Gypsy roles referencing her image as the Queen of Striptease. In 1958 she played a saloon owner in *Screaming Mimi*, which starred Anita Ekberg as a young stripper working at El Madhouse Nightclub in Los Angeles. Gypsy shimmies to the song that Rita Hayworth had made famous in *Gilda*, "Put the Blame on Mame." In 1963 she played "Madame Olga" in *The Stripper*, based on the William Inge play, *A Loss of Roses*, which starred Joanne Woodward as the ingénue.

She did even less well in the theater. In 1960, when Gypsy played *Auntie Mame* on the Straw Hat Circuit, she looked tired.

Wrinkled from gardening in the California sun, she had aged. Plugging comedy more than sex appeal was not new, but some of the gestures Gypsy had relied on—like taking off her wig at the finale—now read as grotesque rather than charming and sexy.

A remarkable bit of miscasting occurred in 1961, when producers Carmen Capalbo and Stanley Chase convinced Gypsy to play Pirate Jenny in a thirty-five-week national tour of Bertolt Brecht's *Threepenny Opera*. They had already enlisted June to direct. On the surface, Gypsy as Pirate Jenny was not a terrible idea. Written in 1928 by Brecht and Kurt Weill, *Threepenny* premiered in New York in 1933, when Gypsy was performing at the Irving Place. By the time Gypsy was cast, Marc Blitzstein's adaptation of *Threepenny* had already run for six years at the Theatre de Lys off-Broadway and starred Lotte Lenya, whom George Davis—her then husband and Gypsy's old friend from Seven Middagh Street—had dragged out of retirement.

Rewrites of Pirate Jenny added a striptease. But that Gypsy was unable to sing Weill's music at a time when Bobby Darin and Louis Armstrong had both done dazzling recordings of it doomed the production even though the stripper offered to supplement Pirate Jenny's wardrobe from her personal costume stock. As she put it, "Rehearsals have been quite an experience especially the day they tried to discover the key I sang in." The show opened in Toronto and closed two weeks later. Gypsy took home a harp instead of her $3,000-a-week salary.

The Saleswoman of Striptease

Gypsy spent much of the last ten years of her life endorsing products. Some campaigns exploited her luxury "striptease" image, such as the 1962 Smirnoff vodka print campaign, in which Gypsy, stuffed into a champagne-colored satin evening gown, holds a lorgnette and winks. "The hostess with the mostess," the copy reads. But Gypsy also hawked pedestrian goods. Her last gig was for Voila Gourmet Dog Food in 1968. The woman who, in her youth, ate dog food on the road was now selling French beef burgundy and Irish kidney stew for esoteric canine breeds. For Gypsy the connection was clear: a passion as well as a charity, the dogs made money for her and fit into the public idea of an aging star's responsibility to take care of less-fortunate creatures. The dogs also fulfilled her most important requirement for a cause: they were a sound decision business-wise.

Just like many of today's over-forty female stars in search of a venue, Gypsy became a star again on television. She hosted her first talk show, the *Gypsy Rose Lee Show*, in 1965, from San Francisco. Her warmth drew out Hollywood and New York luminaries in part because Gypsy did not just gossip: she got Ginger Rogers, Truman Capote, Pearl S. Buck, Omar Sharif, Tammy Grimes, Judy Garland, Michael Caine, Andy Warhol, and Tom

Wolfe to talk about serious things. Gypsy was the friendly ex-stripper next door, accessible and domestic. It is to her credit that she held her own in a male field crowded with eminences like Jack Paar and Johnny Carson.

The Gypsy Rose Lee Show mixed glamour with homespun-ness. The lead-in music "va-va-vooms" as though paving the way to a nightclub circa 1961. Although an ornate chandelier hung from the set's ceiling, Gypsy herself wore an unassuming wardrobe. More important, the *Gypsy Rose Lee Show*—and its spinoffs—helped Gypsy adapt to the 1960s freewheeling, loose-lipped mode. But sometimes she went too far. In 1966, when she announced her cancer diagnosis on the show—broadcast live—the studio "had a fit," as she put it.

The show also helped Gypsy get cast again. Some of these roles celebrated her past, and others took an ironic stance toward it. Often it was enough for her to make an appearance and prove that she had survived. In 1966 she had a walk-on role in *The Pruitts of Southampton*, a sitcom about a wealthy family that suddenly went broke when they were made to pay their back taxes. On the TV sit-com *Batman* the following year she played a newscaster. Finally, Gypsy played herself in *Fractured Flickers*, the spoof of silent films created by Chris Hayward and Jay Ward, who also imagined the Rocky and Bullwinkle cartoon characters.

Throughout her life Gypsy had been most motivated by work. She was always a taskmaster, but toward the end she became even more stern. While writing and sometimes while performing she would rise at five a.m. Her journals from this era include both reprimands and pep talks. "I've worked so hard and I am not at all pleased with the outcome," she noted about one show. Another did not get well reviewed, but "I think I gave a good performance."

A dark mood also emerged: "Facing a blank wall is like facing my future," she wrote. One morning, she "wakes up with a premonition of evil."

But although she was shy and worried that when being interviewed she sounded "like a juke box," in public Gypsy refused to be bullied into common wisdom about herself, burlesque, or striptease. When journalists sought her opinion about the "new" stripping and Broadway "nudicals," like *Hair* and Kenneth Tynan's *Oh! Calcutta!* she did not always give the answer they wanted. In 1966 a reporter tried to corner her into saying that the sexual revolution had made stripteasing obsolete: "I asked what she thought of kids doing those weird dances on TV: bumps and grinds are less offensive with kids than with the older ones. Wasn't that the kind of stuff that killed burlesque? 'No,' said Gyp. 'It was real estate that did that. The burlesque theatres were in the slums and there aren't any slums any more.'"

Gypsy's myth-making intelligence at the end of her life recalls the conclusions she had arrived at years earlier. That she could distinguish between herself and her legend proves her ability to see herself not just as a person but as a *figura*. Her dedication to revising her own story shares the improvisatory verve of a character in the Pirandello play *Six Characters in Search of an Author*, which had premiered in New York shortly before Gypsy arrived there. A more lowbrow comparison might be to reality television shows.

Gypsy never harbored illusions about her success: "Sometimes you have no specific talent. I have a talent for life, for living. Oh, I could have been a second rate actress . . . instead I've channeled my mediocrity." Or: "All people play roles . . . eventually the act you put on becomes such a good one that you convince yourself. . . . What began as pretense finally becomes a reality," she told the *Sunday News* in 1968, two years before she died.

Even after doctors operated on Gypsy for cancer in 1966, she trouped on. Three years later, she traveled at least twice to Vietnam to visit wounded soldiers in small, out-of-the-way hospitals. She brought them "dirty kosher Chinese fortune cookies" containing jokes by Steve Allen, Morey Amsterdam, and herself. She climbed into bed with them and posed, as she described it, like "a sexy grandmother." What about the antiwar effort? a reporter asked. "I think sometimes, those boys feel deserted, left alone, forgotten, because they think we don't support them. Whether we're for or against the war, we've got to support them," she replied.

In 1969, asked by another reporter about her mother, she threw off one of the lines Laurents gave her character. "All I've got to say is that most people aren't as lucky as I was to have a mother who had grit. If it weren't for her, I wouldn't be where I am today."

When Gypsy died a little over a year later, she provided two revelations. One, according to Erik, was the identity of his father. On her deathbed Gypsy told her son, then seventeen, that his father was not her second husband, Alexander Kirkland, as he had always thought, but the movie director Otto Preminger. The other was: she still liked to perform her striptease.

Conclusion

Not having finished the job in her first memoir, June followed with a second volume, *More Havoc* and a one-woman show, *An Unexpected Evening with June Havoc.* Erik's more amused version of events, *Gypsy and Me*, was published in 1984. Whereas Erik bragged that his mother's entire life was fabliaux, June played the role of the aggrieved sister compelled by her superior moral character to "set the record straight." Of these perspectives I find Gypsy's reckless attitude toward the truth to be most charming—a dimension of the American penchant for self-invention and self-aggrandizement. Gypsy didn't sell snake oil. She wasn't deceiving sick people. Her goal was to amuse, to make people laugh.

Even today I am not the only one to forgive Gypsy's dissembling. Today her lies make the corners of our mouths turn up. At first I thought this was simply because lying in showbiz doesn't evoke the same outrage it does in journalism or in memoir of politics. Then I believed Americans tolerate Gypsy because she lied so prettily, never insisting that the listener believe the truth of her story. Then I arrived at the following theory: when you strip away Gypsy's witty veneer, what you get instead of a cracked foundation is a glimpse of the narrow line between self-invention and the tragedy emerging from lost souls. And you find here that, whether or not she is telling the truth, Gypsy is neither a puppet nor someone's wallflower daughter forced to take it off— she is a complex and ravishing creature whose act and life reveal self-invention, poignancy, and street smarts.

Gypsy's explanations of her life appeal not just because she is less modern and psychological than June, but because she is less angry. June's revelation, a quarter century after Rose's death and two decades after the musical, that their mother was a gay alcoholic kleptomaniac and a murderer is less interesting than the fable Gypsy told or the musical hinted at.

Yet until recently, critical interest in the Sondheim musical has continued to focus on Rose and her tyranny. In 2003, on the occasion of Sam Mendes's Broadway revival, the brilliant former theater critic Frank Rich—the heir to Brooks Atkinson's mantle—described *Gypsy* as "one of the most enduring creations in the American theatre," as "the American musical theatre's answer to King Lear" and on a par with *Death of a Salesman* and *Glass Menagerie.* The reason is Rose, whom Rich sees less as a monster than as an uncommon woman. Gypsy and the striptease did not concern him.

Then, four years later, HBO announced the filming of a new drama about Gypsy. Ten years in the making, this drama will star Gypsy, as played by Sigourney Weaver, and not Rose, as played by Ethel Merman. Its source is Erik's memoir, *Gypsy and Me: On the Road and Backstage with Gypsy Rose Lee*, not *Gypsy. Gypsy and Me* begins in 1956, when the stripper and her nine-year-old son were touring the Straw Hat Circuit and Gypsy was writing her memoir, and it moves forward until Gypsy's death. By telling more explicit stories about his mother than the ones that his mother told about Rose, Erik connects Gypsy's pathologies to her mother's. But *Gypsy and Me* is sometimes a less satisfying read than *Gypsy* for an unfair reason: unlike his mother, Erik never becomes a star. And whereas the reviews pointed out that Erik is too nice, *Gypsy* suffers more from lack of distance from the subject. It remains to be seen whether it will make good television.

Ultimately, the meaning of Gypsy's striptease is hard to pin down. Gypsy never took it all off, yet she invented modern striptease. She made it possible for women to strip on television and in nightclubs without being arrested, yet what kind of accomplishment is that? She imagined—or maybe a better word is constructed—an entire genre of popular culture, and by doing so created a new ideal of American womanhood. She exposed Americans' longing for fun and sensuality but also predicted our pathological urge to reveal everything.

Before the term *sex symbol* or its modern apotheosis, Marilyn Monroe, came onto the scene, Gypsy represented what author and social critic Camille Paglia refers to as "the sizzle of outlaw sexuality." Gypsy capitalized on that sizzle and made a lot of money, which outraged some observers.

It still does. In 1997 Frank Rich wrote that the "JonBenets of America are the cultural inheritors of Gypsy Rose Lee, who, unlike her sister, did not have the talent to become either a vaudeville star or legitimate actress and so became a stripper instead." This misses the point. The gods endowed Gypsy with one of the only talents required of a great striptease artist: understanding how one's movements and actions seduce others. This talent rewards the mastery of taking off one's gloves and gracefully walking and swinging one's hips at the same time. Striptease schools notwithstanding, these are not, generally speaking, teachable talents.

Gypsy displayed another American talent, too: the talent of being sexy and funny at the same time. Despite her disavowal of that potent combination, she blended the two attributes and, having begun as an outlaw, used them to get herself to the inner sanctum. Unable because of the times and her own limitations to become a movie star, she settled for being a personality and a brand.

Gypsy not only championed the idea that sex sells, she presented its far-flung possibilities and a casual, indifferent, mischievous striptease. Although we claim—more than ever of late—to crave the star who bares it all, we long for the mystery that Gypsy provided. We want the rush that striptease brings us, the thrill that Gypsy gave us.

But what price are we willing to pay? While we are awash in strippers today, it is hard to think of one who started at the bottom and rose, via teasing and irony, to the top. That is no longer what contemporary American striptease icons are made of.

Acknowledgments

I'd like to thank my stellar editor, Jonathan Brent, for shepherding *Gypsy* from start to finish and for his patience and sense of humor about the subject. Thanks, also, to his assistants, Annelise Finegan and Sarah Miller, each of whose calm and speedy responses made the process sweeter. Newspaper and magazine editors too numerous to name have indulged my obsession with Gypsy over the years, and I thank them for doing so. My agent, Denise Shannon, and her colleague Nanci McCloskey supported the project.

Thanks to Jeffrey Schier, Kent Garber, Nancy Hulnick, and Kathy Barber. And the anonymous readers who improved the manuscript.

Special thanks to Gioia Diliberto, Larry Maslon, and my

mother for reading early drafts. I would like to thank Erik Preminger for his sense of humor and graciousness. And Jonathan Santlofer.

A number of archivists and librarians were helpful during this project, especially Maryann Chach and Mark Schwartz at the Shubert Archive, Jeremy McGraw at the Billy Rose Theatre Collection, the University of Chicago interlibrary loan staff, Scott Landvetter, the staff at the Margaret Herrick Library, Edward Comstock at the USC Cinematic Library in Los Angeles, and Heather Jagman at DePaul. At Yaddo, Lesley Leduc tracked down the details about Gypsy's visit to Marc Blitzstein's studio.

DePaul University provided me with a small grant that helped offset the costs of doing research at the Billy Rose Theatre Collection in 2005, and John Culbert and Dean Corrin at the Theatre School gave me time off during 2005–6 and 2007–8. Part of that time was spent working on this book.

Finally, the corporation of Yaddo and Elaina Richardson have given me the space to work so many times over the past few years that I really cannot fully express my gratitude to them in this space. I will say this: Although I don't use a blue ribbon to type, and I don't sign my notes "The Naked Genius," I hope that this book lives up to the spirit of its subject.

Notes

Gypsy Rose Lee (GRL) Collection, Billy Rose Theatre Collection (BRTC), New York Library for the Performing Arts

Gypsy Rose Lee (GRL) Clippings File, Museum of the City of New York (MCNY)

MHL   Margaret Herrick Library, Academy of Motion Picture Arts and Sciences
MPAA   Motion Picture Archives of America Collections
NYPL   New York Public Library

INTRODUCTION
Particles, Legends, Romance

p. 5 "Particles of eroticism": Barthes, *Mythologies*, 84.
p. 7 "The striptease unconsciously teaches": Eco, *Misreadings*, 31.
p. 7 "Some odd things": Levy, *Female Chauvinistic Pigs*, 2.

ONE
Undressing the Family Romance

p. 10 "The stage is 6 feet": Gypsy to Lee Wright, May 15, 1941, press pack, *G-String Murders*, Harold Rome Biographical Series, Irving S. Gilmore Library, Yale University.

p. 11 "It makes me feel like a heel": Gypsy to Hedda Hopper, n.d., Hedda Hopper Collection, MHL.

p. 12 "As common sense": Flanner, Sub-Series 1, Personal Correspondence, GRL Papers, BRTC.

p. 12 "A comic savagery in her manner": Havoc, *More Havoc*, 96.

p. 12 "Witty, kind, very sensible": McCullers, *Illuminations and Night Glare*, 33.

p. 13 "Why don't you wise up?": Lee, *Gypsy*, 240. *Harper's Magazine*, March 1943.

p. 13 "Men just didn't seem to last very long": Havoc, *Early Havoc*, 28.

p. 13 "She always told that story": interview with Erik Preminger.

p. 15 "The midwife picked you up": ibid., 126.

p. 19 "How could I learn anything": Lee, *Gypsy*, 75.

p. 19 "Brontë and Browning": Preminger, *Gypsy and Me*, 65.

p. 20 "They were all talking about books": Lee, *Gypsy*, 93.

p. 20 "My books had already broken": ibid., 94.

p. 20 "Do you like to read?": ibid., 139.

p. 21 "I knew that everyone": Lee, *Gypsy*, 227.

p. 22 "We're usually on the road": ibid., 2.

p. 23 "Was absolute misery": Gypsy to Hedda Hopper, July 17, 1962, Hedda Hopper Collection, MHL.

p. 23 "Burlesque . . . centered": Gilbert, *American Vaudeville*, 5.

p. 24 "Cigarette butts": Lee, *Gypsy*, 181.

p. 25 "I'm no illusion": ibid., 197.

p. 28 "ten yards of lavender net": Lee, *Gypsy*, caption of photo insert.

T W O

The Queen of Striptease

p. 32 "More ladylike": Lee, *Gypsy*, 252.

p. 33 "All Dressed Up for Burlesque?": *New York Evening Journal*, April 27, 1931, GRL Clippings Files, 1930–1939, BRTC.

p. 33 "She's like a breath": *Zit's Theatrical Weekly*, May 11, 1931, BRTC.

p. 34 "Kidded the lacy underpants off": Collyer, *Burlesque*, 56.

pp. 34–35 "Six proposals of marriage": *New York Evening Graphic*, May 6, 1931, 22.

p. 35 "My baby is innocent and pure": quoted in Havoc, *More Havoc*, 101.

p. 35 "I wasn't naked": ibid., 102; *New York Evening Graphic*, cover, May 23, 1931.

p. 35 "Her river did not run to the sea": Minsky, *Minsky's Burlesque*, 140.

p. 35 "Gypsy Rose Lea has no following locally": *Variety*, September 29, 1931, 54.

p. 36 "He was reborn Irving Wexler": Fried, *The Rise and Fall of the Jewish Gangster in America*, 98.

p. 37 "I fired my first shot": Sobel, *Broadway Heartbeat*, 128.

p. 37 "The meal had scarcely begun": ibid., 129.

p. 38 "Delightfully melodious": *Melody*, GRL Clippings Files, BRTC.

p. 38 "Gypsy Rose Lee's career": unpublished paper on burlesque, Irving Drutman, 1935, Personal Correspondence, GRL Papers, BRTC.

p. 38 "Miss Lee panicked the guests": *New York Woman*, October 7, 1936, GRL Clippings Files, 1930–1939, BRTC.

p. 39 "Our friend is much too pretty for me": Gypsy to Charlotte Seitlin, July 7, 1941, press pack, *G-String Murders*, Irving S. Gilmore Music Library, Yale University.

p. 47 "I'm a Lonesome Little Eve": Lee, *Gypsy*, 296.

p. 49 "Give Me a Lay": ibid., 3.

p. 50 "Gypsy Rose Lee": Mitchell, *My Ears Are Bent*, 56.

p. 51 "A princess": Carl Van Doren to Gypsy, May 25, 1942, f5, b7, GRL Papers, BRTC.

p. 51 "I would like to kiss you": Rags to Gypsy, 1935, B2, f7, GRL Papers, BRTC.

p. 51 "Bum uterus": telegram from Rags to Gypsy, May 22, 1935, B2, f7, GRL Papers, BRTC.

pp. 51–52 "I'll have to come back there": Rags to Gypsy, May 27, 1935, B2, f7, GRL Papers, BRTC.

p. 52 "All she did was off her clothes": *New Yorker*, June 8, 1935, 14.

p. 53 "Gypsy called our theater": *Jewish News Weekly of Northern California*, March 14, 1997.

p. 53 "I want to be a legend": Havoc, *Early Havoc*, 160.

p. 54 "All the stuff they bring in with them": Havoc, *More Havoc*, 96.

p. 55 "Social position is now": Winchell, quoted in Gabler, 185.

p. 56 "Lean, hatchet-faced": *Time*, July 3, 1933.

p. 56 "There must be more to this sex-life": Fiske, *Without Music*, 3.

p. 56 "Clarissa": *Time*, July 3, 1933.

p. 57 "The Artist in burlesque": *New York Times*, Jan 4, 1936, 19.

p. 57 "Mae West of Park Avenue": quoted in Shteir, *Striptease*, 180.

p. 58 "A self-possessed lady": O. O. McIntyre, quoted in Lee, 290–91.

p. 58 "Contain[ing] some of the toughest talk": *Time*, November 4, 1935.

p. 59 "Their poor, misfit selves": Ethan Mordden, *New York Times*, Q & A, April 8, 2007.

p. 60 "Wins you at once": Davis, "Gypsy Rose Lee," 51.

p. 61 "This was a takeoff": Geva quoted in Popular Balanchine, b. 9, binders 1–4. Dance Collection, NYPL.

p. 61 Harvey, quoted in Garis, Robert, *Following Balanchine*, 188.

p. 62 "Tormentedly yearning": *Variety*, July 22, 1936.

p. 66 "Her striptease specialty": *Variety*, September 16, 1936, 53.

p. 66 "Have you the faintest?": lyrics from Ziegfeld Follies of 1936 script, Shubert Archives.

p. 73 "Nothing sensuous," and "I play my striptease for laughs": 1936, GRL Clippings Files, MCNY.

p. 74 "An ethnological dance lesson": Lee, *Gypsy*, 300.

p. 74 "It's said she": 1936, Ziegfeld Follies of 1936 Press Clippings File, Shubert Archives.

pp. 74–75 "She Stoops to Conquer": Otis Chatfield-Taylor, *Town and Country*, October 1936; "Gene Tunney": quoted in Lee, *Gypsy*, 290.

p. 75 "They think I'm some kind of freak": *Colliers*, December 19, 1936, 13.

p. 75 "Installed earphones for the dowagers": *New York World*, November 19, 1936, Ziegfeld Follies of 1936 Press Clippings File, Shubert Archives.

p. 77 "I was slamming": quoted in Shout, "The Musical Theatre of Marc Blitzstein," 414.

p. 77 "To satirize the rich": undated ms., B45, f15, GRL Papers, BRTC.

p. 78 "Don't Put Your Daughter on the Stage": *Variety*, October 28, 1936, GRL Clippings Files, 1930–1939, BRTC.

p. 79 "The bandits adroitly stripped": *New York Times*, November 29, 1936, 12.

p. 80 "Had Miss Lee been robbed": *New York Times*, December 13, 1936, 55.

p. 80 "An advertising man named Reimers": *New Yorker*, November 28, 1936, 10.

p. 81 "Valse Fantastique": *New York Times*, December 5, 1936, 14. This waltz was probably by Korsakov's lesser known contemporary Glazunov, whose romantic ballet *Raymonda* told the story of a good girl in love with a bad guy.

p. 81 "The Duchess of Few Clothes": *Chicago Daily Tribune*, December 13, 1936, 13.

p. 81 "Brief and cold-blooded": *Chicago Daily Tribune*, December 1936.

p. 81 "The future Gypsy Rose Lees": *New York Times*, December 26, 1936, 19.

p. 82 "Streamlined chassis": *Variety*, March 6, 1935, 63.

THREE
To Hollywood and Back

p. 83 "Most prominent woman today": *New York Times*, April 25, 1937, 37.

p. 83 "It will be to Newark": *New York Times*, September 10, 1937, 25.

p. 84 "A young lady who proves": *Daily Worker*, August 26, 1937, quoted in *The Red Decade*, 13.

p. 85 "Stripping is definitely": Congressional Hearings, House Immigration Committee, February 17, 1937.

p. 85 "Really": Ibid.

p. 86 "A stack of 20,000": Gypsy, guest columnist for Walter Winchell, August 28, 1940.

p. 87 "Hollywood Tames Gypsy Rose Lee": *Chicago Daily Tribune*, May 2, 1937, E1.

p. 87 "A case of the jitters": *Chicago Daily Tribune*, May 19, 1937, 21.

p. 87 "Dramatic actress": *Los Angeles Times*.

p. 88 "Exemplar of what has most unfortunately": Breen Collection, MPAA.

p. 88 "Why if she only": *Los Angeles Times*, March 25, 1937, c1.

p. 88 "Bound to disappoint": *Time*, August 16, 1937.

pp. 89–90 "The weakest link": *World Telegram*, May 5, 1937, Ziegfeld Follies of 1936 Clippings Files, Shubert Archives.

p. 90 "Died of an apparent self-inflicted bullet wound": *New York Post*, June 2, 1937, Series One, Sub-Series 1, Personal Correspondence Files, b1, f1, GRL Papers, BRTC.

p. 91 "A lean, hungry wolf": Series One, Sub-Series 1, b2, f8, GRL Papers, BRTC.

p. 91 "The most legitimate publicity": Havoc, *More Havoc*, 195.

p. 91 "Too busy": *Chicago Daily Tribune*, August 18, 1937, 4.

p. 92 "Was changed by a certain Mrs. Hovick": Alexander, *Striptease*, ix–x.

p. 93 "At the request of Miss Augustin's mother": *Los Angeles Times*, November 26, 1937, 3.

p. 94 "I am not at all well": Rose to Gypsy, May 6, 1938, Sub-Series 1, Personal Correspondence, Family Correspondence, B1, f7, GRL Papers, BRTC.

p. 94 "Oil stove": Lester Smith to Gypsy, May 7, 1938, b1, f1, GRL Papers, BRTC.

p. 94 "I was your slave": Rose to Gypsy, May 6, 1938, Series One, Sub-Series 1, Personal Correspondence, Family Correspondence, b1, f9, GRL Papers, BRTC.

p. 94 "I have no desire": Gypsy to Rose, telegram, n.d., Sub-Series 1, b1, f9, GRL Papers, BRTC.

p. 94 "After I'd taken": *Fort Wayne Journal Gazette*, November 6, 1938.

p. 94 "Swell collection of autographs": 1937, *New York Herald Tribune*, GRL Clippings Files, BRTC.

p. 95 "She's been detained": *Variety*, November 12, 1938, GRL Clippings Files, 1930–1939.

p. 96 "Making advances at a timid": *Variety*, December 7, 1938, 45.

pp. 96–97 "I have not come to lift my skirts": Abraham Lincoln Brigade pamphlet, Tamiment Labor Library, Bobst Library, New York University.

p. 97 "Clothes?": ibid.

p. 97 "I'd seen Gypsy Rose Lee": Balliet, *New York Voices*, 147.

p. 97 "Promised": Mrs. Mizzy to Gypsy, December 20, 1938, Series One, Sub-Series 1, b2 f8, GRL Papers, BRTC.

p. 97 "Extreme cruelty": Series One, Sub-Series 1, b23, f3, GRL Papers, BRTC.

p. 98 "I'll bare all if they come": November 26, 1938, GRL Clippings Files, 1930–1939, BRTC.

p. 99 "Come and See Gypsy Rose Lee's": Schaffner, *Salvador Dali's Dream of Venus*, 74.

p. 101 "A wholesome small town farm girl": Mangione, *An Ethnic at Large*, 259.

p. 101 "One of the roughest books": *New York Times*, December 7, 1939, 34.

FOUR

The Rise and Fall of the Striptease Intellectual

p. 104 "I am a practitioner": quoted in Mencken, *The American Language, Supplement I*, 586–87.

p. 105 "Ecdysiast, he calls me": ibid.

p. 105 "One of the great fashionable occasions": Daché, *Talking Through My Hats*, 187.

p. 105 "Someone whistled": ibid., 190.

p. 106 "There she was": ibid., 192.

p. 106 "Bigger than Stalin": quoted in Todd, 64.

p. 107 "*Voos ette aytrainjeer*": *Streets of Paris* script, Shubert Archive.

p. 108 "Tall, sleek and mischievous": *New York Times*, May 20, 1940, 19.

p. 108 "Humor in strip-teasing": *New York Times*, May 20, 1940, 21.

p. 108 "We want to watch": *New Yorker*, June 1, 1940, 19.

p. 110 "Mike picked up the myth machine": Havoc, *More Havoc*, 228.

p. 110 "A stripper who don't strip": Todd, quoted in Collyer, *Burlesque*, 54.

p. 111 "I could think of a lot better things": Henry Miller, *Nightmare Notebook*, n.d.

p. 113 "A sulky, extra sensitive character": Flanner, *Paris Was Yesterday*, xviii.

p. 114 "Odd but it was lively": Seebohm, quoted in Shteir, *New York Times Book Review*, November 10, 1996.

p. 114 "Gypsy did not strip": Untermeyer, quoted in Carr, *Lonely Hunter*, 123.

p. 114 "The Yaddo pallor": Gypsy to Lee Wright, July 7, 1941, F8845, Harold Rome Biographical Series 7b, Irving S. Gilmore Music Library, Yale University.

p. 114 "Frankie is in love": McCullers, *Illumination and Night Glare*, 33.

p. 115 "Came around for meals": MacNeice, *The Strings Are False*, 35.

p. 116 "Mak[ing] with the book words": GRL Press Pack, *The G-String Murders*, Harold Rome Biographical Series, Irving S. Gilmore Music Library, Yale University.

p. 116 "Your mind": November 29, 1940, Correspondence, b3 f8, GRL Papers, BRTC.

p. 116 "I'm lonesome": December 15, 1940, in ibid.

p. 116 "I left too early": Todd to Gypsy, telegram, n.d., Series One, Sub-Series 1, b3, f8, GRL Papers, BRTC.

p. 117 "I'd be out there": quoted in Todd, *A Valuable Property*, 70.

p. 118 "Zip": thanks to Richard Rodgers estate.

p. 118 "Can you draw sweet water": *New York Times* review of *Pal Joey*.

p. 119 The "Striptease Intellectual": *American Mercury*, January 1941, 36.

p. 119 "Phony emotionalism": *Chicago Daily Tribune*, January 2, 1941, 15.

p. 120 "The Naked Genius": February 19, 1941, Gypsy to Lee Wright, January 20, 1941, F8845, Harold Rome Biographical Series, Irving S. Gilmore Music Library, Yale University.

p. 120 "The Girl with the Diamond Studded Navel," Gypsy to Lee Wright, March 5, 1941. Irving S. Gilmore Music Library, Yale University.

p. 120 "You see it takes almost an hour": Gypsy to Lee Wright, July 21, 1941, Irving S. Gilmore Music Library, Yale University.

p. 120 "That annoys *me* too much": Gypsy to Lee Wright, January 20, 1941. Harold Rome Biographical Series, Irving S. Gilmore Music Library, Yale University.

p. 121 "Bob's inferiority complex": June's then husband, Jesse, to Gypsy, February 2, 1941, Series One, Sub-Series 1, b2 f8, GRL Papers, BRTC.

p. 121 "Our men need the money now": June 25, 1941, Temple University Theatre Collection.

p. 123 "Well constructed": Simon and Schuster correspondence, author's private collection.

p. 123 "Talking dog": Laurents, *Original Story*, 379.

p. 123 "Isn't even *Crime and Punishment*": Gypsy, 1941, review of her own book, "Down the Aisle" column. GRL Papers.

p. 124 "With eyebrows raised": *New Yorker*, October, 11, 1941.

p. 124 "Readable": *Chicago Daily Tribune*, October 26, 1941, Series One, Sub-Series 1, b1, f8, GRL Papers, BRTC.

p. 124 "A stunt": *Daily Worker*, October 22, 1941.

p. 124 "As American as hot dogs": *New York Times*, March 22, 1942, xi.

p. 124 "Gypsy Rose Lee has not only": *New York Herald Tribune*, n.d., *Star and Garter* publicity files, Shubert Archives.

p. 125 "God is love": October 7, 1943, Series One, Sub-Series 1, b1, f10, GRL Papers, BRTC.

p. 126 "I'd be a dope to play": n.d., GRL Papers, BRTC.

p. 128 "Prim": clipping, January 17, 1960, Temple University Theatre Collection.

p. 128 "Is this a war": *Chicago Daily Tribune*, February 8, 1942, 1.

p. 133 "The poor man has been robbed": Damon Runyon column, September 30, 1942, *New York Herald Tribune*.

p. 134 "Hardly suitable as a husband": Guggenheim, *Confessions of an Art Addict*, 271.

p. 135 "We are glad to note": *New York Times*, October 25, 1942.

p. 137 "If she's an artist": *New York Times*, January 6, 1943, 23.

p. 137 "Idolized": John Cage, video interview, Dallas Public Library Cable Access Studio, 1987.

p. 138 "I miss you": telegram, January 24, 1943. Correspondence, B3, f8, GRL Papers, BRTC.

p. 139 "Does a striptease": *New York Times*, May 14, 1943, 21.

p. 139 "Without actually doing so": GRL Papers.

p. 142 "The Great Private Oshins": *New York Times*, July 29, 1943.

p. 142 "Ironic isn't it": script of *The G-String Murders*, b43, f1–6, GRL Papers, BRTC.

p. 143 "No one expected": *Boston Post*, September 1943, GRL Clippings Files, 1940–1949, BRTC.

p. 143 "A polite bore": *New York Times*, November 7, 1943, xi.

p. 143 "With all due respect": *New York Times*, January 1, 1945.

p. 144 "You've got to show the boys": *Chicago Daily Tribune*, June 18, 1943, 21.

p. 144 "You say you can": letter from Gypsy to Todd, n.d., B44, f7, GRL Papers, BRTC.

p. 145 "A sample book": *Time*, January 1943, Dorothy Wheelock folder, b23, f5, GRL Papers. BRTC.

p. 146 "Anyone who writes": April 13, 1942, GRL Clippings Files, 1940–1949, BRTC.

p. 147 "Gypsy's Growing Pains," July 15, 1944, *New York Journal American*, GRL Clippings Files, 1940–1949, BRTC.

p. 147 "She used to make dinners": Preminger, *Gypsy and Me*, 258.

p. 148 "This is a period picture": *Belle of the Yukon* Press File, MHL.

pp. 148–149 "Time. Diamond bracelets": Quote from *Belle of the Yukon*.

p. 149 "Her usual earthiness and humor": *New York Times*, March 30, 1945, 18.

p. 149 "Can't you write about other people?": Rose to Gypsy, August 18, 1945, Series One, Sub-Series 1, b1, f12, GRL Papers, BRTC.

p. 150 "Current time magazine": telegram, Craig Rice to Gypsy, January 24, 1946, B7, f10, GRL Papers, BRTC.

FIVE

Selling Striptease

p. 151 "Startled televiewers": *Time*, October 4, 1948.

pp. 151–152 "There were no technical difficulties": *Chicago Daily Tribune*, October 24, 1948, SW14.

p. 152 "So I'd have something to take off": quoted in *Chicago Daily Tribune*, March 31, 1950, A10.

p. 153 "Were she as high": letter from "monkey girl" to Hedda Hopper, n.d., Hedda Hopper Collection, MHL.

p. 153 "I can hardly wait": letter from Gypsy to Hedda, n.d., in ibid.

p. 154 "In practically every exhibit": ibid.

p. 154 "Fairy godmother in a Cinderella striptease": *Variety*, September 7, 1949, 56.

p. 155 "City chicken": *New York World-Telegram*, September 17, 1937, GRL Clippings Files, 1930–1939, BRTC.

p. 157 "Gypsy Rose Lee": *Variety*, January 10, 1951, 54.

p. 157 "Harry Truman": Preminger, *Gypsy and Me*, 205.

p. 158 "A dear and close associate": quoted in *Time*, September 20, 1950.

p. 158 "Look at me": ibid.; *Post*, September 14, 1950, Temple University Theatre Collection.

p. 159 "No actor should join": draft of editorial, Series One, Sub-Series 2, B7, f5, GRL Papers, BRTC.

p. 160 "He met a beautiful girl": *New York Mirror*, July 16, 1957, GRL Clippings Files, 1950–1959, BRTC.

p. 161 *"What Are Your Dreams?"*: b14, f13, GRL Papers, BRTC.

p. 161 "I am not cut out": n.d., GRL Clippings Files, 1950–1959, BRTC.

p. 161 "It was a very beautiful occasion": *New York Mirror*, July 15, 1957, GRL Clippings Files, 1950–1959, BRTC.

p. 161 "Strangled her": GRL Papers, BRTC.

p. 162 "The first year of marriage": *The American Weekly*, January 17, 1960, GRL Clippings Files, 1960–1969, BRTC.

p. 162 "Haven't heard anything": letter from Gypsy to June Havoc, June 6, 1951, Series One, Sub-Series 1, B1, f5, GRL Papers, BRTC.

p. 162 "Mother died at 6:30": draft of letter, January 2, 1954, Appointment Calendars, Series Two, Sub-Series 1, GRL Papers, BRTC.

p. 162 "Speak well of all": Series Two, Sub-Series 1, GRL Papers, BRTC.

p. 162 "Mike was killed": March 22, 1958, in ibid.

p. 163 "And what about wired brassieres?": "Formfit Talk," Plaza Hotel Luncheon, April 26, 1950, Hedda Hopper Collection, MHL, MPAA.

p. 163 "You love those slow burning": Series One, Sub-Series 2, f17, b6, GRL Papers, BRTC.

p. 164 "Jeep among limousines": quoted in Flinn, *Brass Diva*, 285.

p. 164 "Audiences watch me": May 15, 1951, Series Two, Sub-Series 1, GRL Papers, BRTC.

p. 164 "At one stage": *New York Herald Tribune*, September 12, 1951, Temple University Theatre Collection.

p. 168 "Her clever remarks": *Saturday Review*, May 25, 1957, GRL Clippings Files, 1950–1959.

p. 168 "The story of a woman": Laurents, *Original Story*, 376.

p. 169 "Reads book reviews": Laurents and Styne, *Gypsy*, 101.

p. 169 "I must not play Casa Cugat": April 5, 1959, f1, b12, GRL Papers, BRTC.

p. 169 "Oh darling, I've given": Laurents, *Original Story*, 379.

p. 170 "I don't mind working": Series xi, Sub-Series 2, GRL Papers, BRTC.

p. 170 "Too chaste in demeanor": *New Yorker*, May 29, 1959, 65.

p. 171 "You can't sell sex": op. cit.

p. 172 "We are all absolutely convinced": quoted in Jowitt, *Jerome Robbins*, 325.

p. 172 "Mama, I'm Pretty": Laurents and Styne, *Gypsy*, 94.

p. 173 "My mother": Laurents and Styne, *Gypsy*, 96.

p. 173 "I can't think of Rose": Appointment Calendars, n.d., Series Two, Sub-Series 1, Personal Papers, 1936–1971, GRL Papers, BRTC.

p. 173 "Mastodon": Kerr, May 22, 1959, in *New York Theatre Critics Reviews, 1959*, 301.

p. 174 "A nightmare incarnation": Kenneth Tynan, *New Yorker*, May 30, 1959, 65.

p. 174 "Juggernaut": Brooks Atkinson review, *New York Times*, May 22, 1959, xi.

p. 174 "Folklore doesn't become": *New Yorker*, May 9, 1961, 188.

p. 174 "We love you, Gypsy": *New York Times*, May 10, 1961, 53.

p. 175 "It was like an Italian palazzo": Interview with Barbara Preminger, August 10, 2008.

p. 175 "unworldly": Interview with David Patrick Columbia, June 10, 2008.

p. 179 "Rehearsals have been": Gypsy to Hedda Hopper, September 11, 1961, Hedda Hopper Collection, MHL, MPAA.

p. 181 "Had a fit": November 22, 1966, Temple University Theatre Collection.

p. 182 "I've worked so hard": Appointment Calendars, n.d., GRL, BRTC.

p. 182 "Like a juke box": Appointment Calendars, Series One, Sub-Series 2, GRL Papers, BRTC.

p. 182 "I asked what she thought": *New Yorker,* January 15, 1966, GRL Clippings Files, BRTC.

p. 183 "Sometimes you have no specific talent": *New York Post,* January 16, 1966, GRL Clippings Files, 1960–1969, BRTC.

p. 183 "Dirty kosher Chinese fortune cookies": *Los Angeles Times,* January 13, 1969. g1.

p. 183 "I think sometimes": GRL Papers, BRTC.

p. 183 "All people play roles": *Sunday News,* July 23, 1968, 25s.

p. 184 "All I've got to say": *Charlotte News,* 1963, b6, f9, GRL Papers, BRTC.

Conclusion

p. 187 "One of the most enduring": Frank Rich, *New York Times,* May 4, 2003, ARi.

p. 188 "The sizzle of outlaw sexuality": Paglia, column in *Salon,* November 11, 1997.

p. 188 "JonBenets of America": Frank Rich, *New York Times,* January 18, 1997, 23.

Bibliography

Primary Sources

Gypsy Rose Lee (GRL) Collection, Billy Rose Theatre Collection (BRTC), New York Library for the Performing Arts

Gypsy Rose Lee (GRL) Clippings File, Museum of the City of New York

Academy of Motion Pictures Arts and Sciences Library, Margaret Herrick Motion Picture Archive

Hedda Hopper Collection

Motion Picture Archives of America Collections (MPAA)

    Babes in Baghdad

    You Can't Have Everything

    Ali Baba

    Battle of Broadway

    Sally, Irene, and Mary

    My Lucky Star

    Lady of Burlesque

    Stage Door Canteen

    Doll Face

    Ball of Fire

USC Cinematic Arts Library

20th Century Fox Collection, Darryl Zanuck memos

Western Historical Manuscript Collection
Shubert Archives:
 Follies of 1936 clippings file
 Follies of 1936 contract file
 Streets of Paris clippings file
 Streets of Paris contract file
Irving S. Gilmore Music Library, Yale University
 Harold Rome Biographical Series
Yaddo Archives

Secondary Sources

Allen, Robert. *Horrible Prettiness: Burlesque and American Culture.* Chapel Hill: University of North Carolina Press, 1991.

Atkinson, Brooks. *Broadway.* New York: Macmillan, 1974.

———. *Broadway Scrapbook.* New York: Macmillan, 1947.

Balliett, Whitney. *New York Voices: 27 Portraits by Whitney Balliett.* Jackson: University Press of Mississippi, 2006.

Barthes, Roland. *Mythologies.* New York: Farrar, Straus, and Giroux, 1957.

Bergreen, Laurence. *As Thousands Cheer: The Life of Irving Berlin.* New York: Da Capo, 1996.

Black, Gregory. *Hollywood Censored, Morality Codes, Catholics, and the Movies.* Cambridge: Cambridge University Press, 1996.

Bowles, Jane. *Feminine Wiles.* Santa Barbara, Calif.: Black Sparrow, 1976.

———. *Out in the World: Selected Letters of Jane Bowles, 1935–1970.* Edited by Millicent Dillon. Santa Rosa, Calif.: Black Sparrow, 1990.

Bowles, Paul. *In Touch: The Letters of Paul Bowles.* Edited by Jeffrey Miller. New York: Flamingo, 1995.

———. *Without Stopping: An Autobiography.* Hopewell, N.J.: Ecco, 1972.

Britten, Benjamin. *Letters from a Life: Selected Letters and Diaries of Benjamin Britten.* Volume 1, 1929–1939, and Volume 2, 1939–45. Edited by Donald Mitchell and Philip Reed. Berkeley: University of California Press, 1991.

Bucknell, Katherine, and Nicholas Jenkins, eds. *"In Solitude, for Company": W. H. Auden After 1940: Unpublished Prose and Recent Criticism.* Auden Studies 3. Oxford: Clarendon, 1994.

Cage, John. Interview, 1987, Dallas Public Library Cable Access Studio, Dallas, Texas.

Capote, Truman. *Answered Prayers: The Unfinished Novel.* New York: Vintage, 1994.

Carr, Virginia Spencer. *Lonely Hunter: A Biography of Carson McCullers.* New York: Doubleday, 1975.

Chauncey, George. *Gay New York: Gender, Urban Culture, and the Makings of the Gay Male World: 1890–1940.* New York: Basic, 1994.

Cocteau, Jean. *Around the World Again in Eighty Days.* London: Tauris-Parke Paperbacks, 2000.

Cohn, Art. *The Nine Lives of Michael Todd.* New York: Random House, 1958.

Collyer, Martin. *Burlesque.* New York: Lancer, 1964.

Daché, Lily. *Talking Through My Hats.* New York: Coward-McCann, 1946.

Davidson, Susan, and Phillip Rylands, eds. *Peggy Guggenheim and Frederick Kiesler: The Story of Art of This Century.* New York: Guggenheim Books, 2004.

Davis, George. "Gypsy Rose Lee: The Dark Young Pet of Burlesque." *Vanity Fair* (February 1936): 51–53.

Drutman, Irving. *Good Company: A Memoir Mostly Theatrical.* Boston: Little, Brown, 1976.

Duberman, Martin. *The World of Lincoln Kirstein.* New York: Alfred A. Knopf, 2007.

Eco, Umberto. *Misreadings.* San Diego: Harcourt Brace, 1993.

Erskine, John. "Burlesque Ritual." *Stage* (October 1936): 58–59.

Fiske, Dwight. *Why Should Penguins Fly? And Other Stories.* London: Robert Hale, 1934.

———. *Without Music.* New York: Chatham, 1933.

Flanner, Janet. *Paris Was Yesterday, 1925–1939.* Edited by Irving Drutman. New York: Viking, 1972.

Gabler, Neal. *Walter Winchell: Gossip, Power, and the Culture of Celebrity.* New York: Knopf, 1995.

Garebian, Keith. *The Making of Gypsy.* New York: Mosaic, 1998.

Garis, Robert. *Following Balanchine.* New Haven: Yale University Press, 1997.

Gelenter, David. *1939: The Lost World of the Fair.* New York: Free Press, 1995.

Gilbert, Douglas. *American Vaudeville: Its Life and Times.* New York: Whittlesly House, 1940.

Gopnik, Adam. "The Naked City: The New Burlesque vs. The Old Smut." *New Yorker* (July 23, 2001).

Gordon, Eric A. *Making a Mark: The Life and Music of Marc Blitzstein.* New York: St. Martin's, 1989.

Gottlieb, Polly. *The Nine Lives of Billy Rose.* New York: Crown, 1968.

Greenberg, Clement. "Avant-garde and Kitsch." *Partisan Review* 6 (Fall 1939): 34–39.

Guggenheim, Peggy, ed. *Art of This Century: Objects, Drawings, Photographs, Sculptures, Collages, 1910–1942.* New York: Arno Press, 1942.

———. *Out of This Century: Confessions of an Art Addict.* New York: Ecco, 1997.

Hare, David, ed. *VVV.* New York: March, 1943.

Havoc, June. *Early Havoc.* New York: Simon and Schuster, 1959.

———. *More Havoc.* New York: Harper Collins, 1980.

Jacobs, Laura. "Taking It All Off." *Vanity Fair* (March 2003): 198, 203–4, 206–8, 210–12, 217, 219, 220.

Jowitt, Deborah. *Jerome Robbins, His Life, His Dance, His Theatre.* New York: Simon and Schuster, 2004.

Koestenbaum, Wayne. *The Queen's Throat: Opera, Homosexuality, and the Mystery of Desire.* New York: Poseidon, 1993.

Lahr, Bert. *Notes on a Cowardly Lion: A Biography of Bert Lahr.* Berkeley: University of California Press, 2000.

Laurents, Arthur. *Original Story by: A Memoir of Broadway and Hollywood.* New York: Knopf, 2000.

Laurents, Arthur, and Jule Styne. *Gypsy.* New York: Theatre Communications Group, 2003.

Lears, Jackson. *Fables of Abundance: A Cultural History of Advertising in America.* New York: Basic, 1994.

Lee, Gypsy Rose. *The G-String Murders.* New York: Simon and Schuster, 1942.

———. *Gypsy: A Memoir.* New York: Harper, 1957.

———. *Mother Finds a Body.* New York: Simon and Schuster, 1942.

Lerman, Leo. *The Grand Surprise: The Journals of Leo Lerman.* New York: Knopf, 2007.

Levy, Ariel. *Female Chauvinistic Pigs: Women and Raunch Culture.* New York: Free Press, 2006.

Lewis, Frederick Allen. *Only Yesterday: An Informal History of the Twenties.* New York: Hill and Wang, 1929.

Liepe-Levinson, Katherine. *Strip Show: Performances of Gender and Desire.* New York: Routledge, 2002.

Lyons, Eugene. *The Red Decade: The Stalinist Penetration of America.* Indianapolis: Bobbs-Merrill, 1941.

MacNeice, Louis. *The Strings Are False: An Unfinished Biography.* New York: Oxford University Press, 1966.

Mangione, Jerre. *An Ethnic at Large: A Memoir of America in the Thirties and Forties.* Philadelphia: Pennsylvania University Press, 1978.

McCullers, Carson. *Illumination and Night Glare*. Madison: University of Wisconsin Press, 1998.

———. *The Member of the Wedding*. Boston: Houghton Mifflin, 1946.

McNair, Brian. *Striptease Culture: Sex, Media, and the Democratization of Desire*. New York: Routledge, 2002.

Mencken, H. L. *The American Language, Supplement I*. New York: Knopf, 1945.

Meredith, Scott. *George S. Kaufman and His Friends*. New York: Doubleday, 1974.

Michaels, Leonard. "The Zipper." In *The Best American Essays*, edited by Susan Sontag. New York: Ticknor & Fields, 1992.

Miller, D. A. *Place for Us (Essay on the Broadway Musical)*. Cambridge, Mass.: Harvard University Press, 1998.

Miller, Henry. *Aller Retour New York*. New York: New Directions, 1959.

———. *The Books in My Life*. New York: New Directions, 1969.

Minsky, Mort. *Minsky's Burlesque: A Fast and Funny Look at America's Bawdiest Era*. New York: Arbor House, 1986.

Mitchell, Joseph. *My Ears Are Bent*. New York: Panthcon, 2001.

Mordden, Ethan. *All That Glittered: The Golden Age of Drama on Broadway, 1919–1959*. New York: St. Martin's, 2007.

———. *Better Foot Forward: The History of the American Musical Theatre*. New York: Viking, 1976.

———. *Coming Up Roses: The Broadway Musical in the 1950s*. New York: Oxford University Press, 1998.

Nathan, George Jean. *The Art of the Night*. New York: Knopf, 1928.

———. *Entertainment of a Nation, Or Three Sheets to the Wind*. New York: Knopf, 1942.

Norse, Harold. *Memoirs of a Bastard Angel: A Fifty-Year Literary and Erotic Odyssey*. New York: Thunder's Mouth, 1989.

Page, Tim. *Dawn Powell: A Biography*. New York: Henry Holt, 1998.

———, ed. *Selected Letters of Dawn Powell, 1913–1965*. New York: Henry Holt, 1988.

Paglia, Camille. *Sexual Personae, Art and Decadence from Nefertiti to Emily Dickinson*. New Haven: Yale University Press, 1990.

Preminger, Erik. *Gypsy and Me: On the Road and at Home with Gypsy Rose Lee*. New York: Frog, 1974.

Rome, Harold. *Pins and Needles*. Columbia Masterworks, New York, 1962. Compact Disk.

Rosenberg, Deena. *Fascinating Rhythm: The Collaboration of George and Ira Gershwin*. Ann Arbor: University of Michigan Press, 1998.

Savigneau, Joseyanne. *Carson McCullers: A Life*. New York: Houghton Mifflin, 2001.

Schaffner, Ingrid. *Dream of Venus: The Surrealist Funhouse from the 1939 Fair*. New York: Princeton Architectural Press, 2002.

Schickel, Richard. *The Stars: The Personalities Who Made the Movies*. New York: Dial, 1962.

Seebohm, Caroline. "Conscripts to an Age." Unpublished essay. Britten-Pears Library, Aldeburgh, United Kingdom.

Senelick, Laurence. *The Changing Room, Sex Drag and Theatre*. New York: Routledge, 1999.

Shout, John D. "The Musical Theatre of Marc Blitzstein." *American Music* 3, no. 4 (Winter 1985): 413–28.

Shteir, Rachel. *Striptease: The Untold History of the Girlie Show*. New York: Oxford University Press, 2004.

Siegel, Marcia. *The Shapes of Change: Images of American Dance*. Berkeley: University of California Press, 1979.

Snyder, Robert. *The Voice of the City: Vaudeville and Popular Culture in New York*. New York: Oxford University Press, 1989.

Sobel, Bernard. *Broadway Heartbeat: Memoirs of a Press Agent*. New York: Hermitage House, 1953.

———. *A Pictorial History of Burlesque*. New York: Bonanza, 1956.

Solomon, William. *Literature, Amusement, and Technology in the Great Depression*. New York: Cambridge University Press, 2002.

Taylor, Theodore. *Jule: The Story of Composer Jule Styne*. New York: Random House, 1979.

Tippins, Sherill. *February House: The Story of W. H. Auden, Carson McCullers, Jane and Paul Bowles*. New York: Houghton Mifflin, 2005.

Todd, Michael, Jr. *Valuable Property: The Life Story of Mike Todd*. New York: Arbor House, 1983.

Tynan, Kenneth. *Curtains: Selections from Drama Criticism and Related Writings*. New York: Atheneum, 1961.

Vreeland, Diana. *D. V.* New York: Da Capo, 2003.

Watts, Jill. *Mae West: An Icon in Black and White*. New York: Oxford University Press, 2001.

Williams, John A., and Dorothy Sterling. *Richard Wright: A Biography*. New York: Putnam's, 1968.

Williams, Tennessee. *Selected Letters, Volume Two: 1945–1957*. New York: New Directions, 2002.

Index

Vertes, Marcel, 115, 136
Victory Book Campaign, 124
Vietnam War, 183
Voila Gourmet Dog Food, 180
Vreeland, Diana, 108, 132

war bonds, 121
Watters, George Manker, 100
Weaver, Sigourney, 9, 187
Weidman, Jerome, 125
Weill, Kurt, 113, 179
West, Mae, 48, 57, 59–60, 86, 87, 88–89, 148, 156, 176
Wexler, Irving, 36–37
Whalen, Grover, 99
What Makes You Tick?, 158
What's My Line?, 159
Wheelock, Dorothy, 145

White, George, 37–38
Wilder, Billy, 126, 127
Wilson, Edmund, 23
Winchell, Walter, 55, 73, 90, 108
Wolf, Louise Dahl, 113
The Women, 156
Wood, Natalie, 170
World Telegram, 50, 105
Wright, Lee, 119, 120, 125, 144

Yaddo, 101, 111, 113
You Can't Have Everything, 87, 88, 89

Zanuck, Darryl, 86, 87, 88, 91, 92
Ziegfeld, Florenz, 36–37
Ziegfeld Follies (1936), 62–73, *64*, 81
zippers, 46–47, 98

Credits

Quotations from the Gypsy Rose Lee Papers are used with permission of Erik Lee Preminger.

Excerpts from *Gypsy: Memoirs of America's Most Celebrated Stripper,* by Gypsy Rose Lee, published by Frog, Ltd., copyright © 1985 by Erik Lee Preminger. Reprinted with permission of publisher.

Excerpts from *My G-String Mother: At Home and Backstage with Gypsy Rose Lee,* by Erik Lee Preminger, published by Frog, Ltd., copyright 2004 by Erik Lee Preminger. Reprinted with permission of publisher.

Selection from pp. 96, 102, 160, 195, 228, 276 from *More Havoc,* by June Havoc, copyright © 1979 by June Havoc. Reprinted by permission of HarperCollins Publishers.

Quotations from Carson McCullers used with permission of the Estate of Carson McCullers.

Excerpt from "The Socratic Strip," in *Misreadings,* by Umberto Eco, copyright © 1963 by Arnoldo Mondadori Editore S.p.A. Milano, English translation copyright © 1993 by Harcourt, Inc. and Jonathan Cape Limited, reprinted by permission of Houghton Mifflin Harcourt Publishing Company.

Excerpt from the song "Zip" by Richard Rodgers and Lorenz Hart, copyright © 1951 and 1962 by Chappell & Co. Inc. Copyright Renewed. Copyright

Assigned to Williamson Music and WB Music Corp. for the extended renewal period of copyright in the USA. International Copyright Secured. All Rights Reserved. Used by permission.

Quotations from *Gypsy: A Musical Fable*, copyright © 1959, 1960, renewed 1989 by Arthur Laurents, Gypsy Rose Lee, and Stephen Sondheim. Published by Theatre Communications Group. Reprinted with permission of the publisher.

Quotation of letter from Arthur Laurents to Jerome Robbins during a rehearsal of *Gypsy* reprinted with permission of Arthur Laurents.

Quotation from *The Rise and Fall of the Jewish Gangster*, by Alfred Fried. Copyright © 1994 Columbia University Press. Reprinted with permission of the publisher.

Excerpt by Henry Miller, from *Aller Retour New York*, copyright © 1991 by Barbara Sylvas Miller, Henry Tony Miller, and Valentine Miller, copyright © 1991 by New Directions Publishing Corp. Reprinted by permission of New Directions Publishing Corp.

Excerpt by Henry Miller, from *The Books in My Life*, copyright © 1969 by New Directions Publishing Corp. Reprinted by permission of New Directions Publishing Corp.

Excerpt from *Mythologies*, by Roland Barthes, published by Jonathan Cape. Reprinted by permission of The Random House Group Ltd.

Franklin Pierce University

00190142

DUE